HENRI J. M. NOUWEN

✠

SHOW ME THE WAY

Readings for Each Day of Lent

CROSSROAD • NEW YORK

1994

The Crossroad Publishing Company
370 Lexington Avenue, New York, NY 10017

Printed in the United States of America
Typesetting output: TEXSource, Houston

Library of Congress Cataloging-in-Publication Data
Nouwen, Henri J. M.
    [Zeige mir den Weg. English]
    Show me the way : readings for each day of Lent / Henri J.M.
Nouwen.
    p. cm.
    Translation: of Zeige mir den Weg.
    ISBN 0-8245-1029-1; 0-8245-1353-3 (pbk.)
    1. Lent—Prayer-books and devotions—English. 2. Lent—
Meditations. I. Title.
BX2170.L4N68 1992
242'.34—dc20
                                        91-35755
                                         CIP

❧ Acknowledgments ❧

We wish to acknowledge the following publishers for permission to reprint previously published material.

From *Compassion* by Henri J.M. Nouwen, D. Morrison, and D. McNeill. Copyright © 1982 by Donald P. McNeill, Douglas A. Morrison, and Henri J.M. Nouwen. Used by permission of Doubleday, a division of Bantam Doubleday Dell Publishing Group, Inc.

From *Creative Ministry* by Henri J.M. Nouwen. Copyright © 1971 by Henri J.M. Nouwen. Used by permission of Doubleday, a division of Bantam Doubleday Dell Publishing Group, Inc.

From *A Cry for Mercy* by Henri J.M. Nouwen. Copyright © 1981 by Henri J.M. Nouwen. Used by permission of Doubleday, a division of Bantam Doubleday Dell Publishing Group, Inc. and by permission of Gill and Macmillan Publishers, Dublin.

From *The Genesee Diary* by Henri J.M. Nouwen. Copyright © 1976 by Henri J.M. Nouwen. Used by permission of Doubleday, a division of Bantam Doubleday Dell Publishing Group, Inc.

Excerpts from *Gracias! A Latin American Journal* by Henri J.M. Nouwen. Copyright © 1983 by Henri J.M. Nouwen. Reprinted by permission of HarperCollins Publishers.

Excerpts from *Heart Speaks to Heart* by Henri J.M. Nouwen. Copyright © 1989 by Ave Maria Press, Notre Dame, IN 46556. All rights reserved. Used with permission of the publisher.

Excerpts from *A Letter of Consolation* by Henri J.M. Nouwen. Copyright © 1982 by Henri J.M. Nouwen. Reprinted by permission of HarperCollins Publishers.

Excerpts from *Letters to Marc* by Henri J.M. Nouwen. Copyright © 1987, 1988 by Henri J.M. Nouwen. English translation copyright © 1988 by Harper & Row, Publishers, Inc. and Darton,

❧ Contents ❧

⊸❦ Foreword ❧⊷

"Show me your way, O Lord!" The longing expressed in the Psalms (see 25:4; 27:11; 86:11) by the soul seeking God is the same urgent call heard today from people who have entered on the pilgrim's road of faith. Many have described this road and made it clear that it is no broad avenue, but a narrow path leading to the "gate of life" (see Matt. 7:13).

The "search for the way" is a recurrent theme in Henri Nouwen's books, which are road signs pointing to decisive commitment, to deep love of God and our fellow men and women. In those books silence and prayer emerge as the place and breath of faith; conversion and renewal, painful leave-taking and bold new beginnings appear as way stations for opening ourselves again and again to the urgency of love. Christian life on this road is never closed up. It continually realizes itself amid the world, in deeds of love, in creative activity for people.

The way through Lent comprises "putting aside the works of darkness," "putting on the works of light," and the daily exercise in prayer. As Henri Nouwen, a master of prayer, says, "Praying means above all listening to the voice of Jesus, who dwells in the depths of the heart. Jesus does not force himself on us, his voice is reserved. Whatever we may do in our lives, let us never fail to listen to the voice of the Lord in our hearts. Because in our restless, noisy world the loving voice of God is easily drowned out. Each day let's keep a certain period of time free for this active listening to God, even if it's only ten minutes. Spending ten minutes every day exclusively on Jesus can change our lives from the ground up."

The texts in this anthology, chosen from the works of Henri Nouwen (see p. 141), aim to prompt and guide the

9

reader for such a period of prayer and recollection. As a Lenten handbook it presents the man or woman at prayer with *God's Word* in a brief text from the liturgical reading or the Gospel of the day in question. The *Meditation* that follows leads into the reality of one's own life and to the translation of faith into reality that is summed up in a concluding *Prayer*.

May this Lenten book serve as an invitation to dare once more to take the Easter path of following Christ.

F. JOHNA

SHOW ME THE WAY

✠

⊰⊹ Ash Wednesday ⊹⊱

"I shall judge each of you by what that person does — declares the Lord Yahweh. Repent, renounce all your crimes, avoid all occasions for guilt. Shake off all the crimes you have committed, and make yourselves a new heart and a new spirit! Why die, House of Israel? I take no pleasure in the death of anyone — declares the Lord Yahweh — so repent and live!"

—Ezek. 18:30–32

The Lenten season begins. It is a time to be with you in a special way, a time to pray, to fast, and thus to follow you on your way to Jerusalem, to Golgotha, and to the final victory over death.

I am still so divided. I truly want to follow you, but I also want to follow my own desires and lend an ear to the voices that speak about prestige, success, human respect, pleasure, power, and influence. Help me to become deaf to these voices and more attentive to your voice, which calls me to choose the narrow road to life.

I know that Lent is going to be a very hard time for me. The choice for your way has to be made every moment of my life. I have to choose thoughts that are your thoughts, words that are your words, and actions that are your actions. There are no times or places without choices. And I know how deeply I resist choosing you.

Please, Lord, be with me at every moment and in every place. Give me the strength and the courage to live this season faithfully, so that, when Easter comes, I will be able to taste with joy the new life which you have prepared for me. Amen.

13

God's mercy is greater than our sins. There is an awareness of sin that does not lead to God but to self-preoccupation. Our temptation is to be so impressed by our sins and failings and so overwhelmed by our lack of generosity that we get stuck in a paralyzing guilt. It is the guilt that says: "I am too sinful to deserve God's mercy." It is the guilt that leads to introspection instead of directing our eyes to God. It is the guilt that has become an idol and therefore a form of pride. Lent is the time to break down this idol and to direct our attention to our loving Lord. The question is: "Are we like Judas, who was so overcome by his sin that he could not believe in God's mercy any longer and hanged himself, or are we like Peter who returned to his Lord with repentance and cried bitterly for his sins?" The season of Lent, during which winter and spring struggle with each other for dominance, helps us in a special way to cry out for God's mercy.

Prayer

Faithful God, trusting in you,
we begin
the forty days of conversion and penance.
Give us the strength for Christian discipline,
that we may renounce evil
and be decisive in doing good.
We ask this through Jesus Christ.

❧ Thursday after Ash Wednesday ❧

Choose life, then, so that you and your descendants may live, in the love of Yahweh your God, obeying his voice, holding fast to him; for in this your life consists.

—Deut. 30:19–20

✠

A life of faith is a life of gratitude — it means a life in which I am willing to experience my complete dependence upon God and to praise and thank him unceasingly for the gift of being. A truly eucharistic life means always saying thanks to God, always praising God, and always being more surprised by the abundance of God's goodness and love. How can such a life not also be a joyful life? It is the truly converted life in which God has become the center of all. There gratitude is joy and joy is gratitude and everything becomes a surprising sign of God's presence.

✠

Whenever Jesus says to the people he has healed: "Your faith has saved you," he is saying that they have found new life because they have surrendered in complete trust to the love of God revealed in him. Trusting in the unconditional love of God: that is the way to which Jesus calls us. The more firmly you grasp this, the more readily will you be able to perceive why there is so much suspicion, jealousy, bitterness, vindictiveness, hatred, violence, and discord in our world. Jesus himself interprets this by comparing God's love to the light. He says:

> . . . though the light has come into the world
> people have preferred
> darkness to light
> because their deeds were evil.

15

And indeed, everybody who does wrong
hates the light and avoids it,
to prevent his actions from being shown up;
but whoever does the truth
comes out into the light,
so that what he is doing may plainly appear as done
  in God.

Jesus sees the evil in this world as a lack of trust in God's
love. He makes us see that we persistently fall back on
ourselves, rely more on ourselves than on God, and are
inclined more to love of self than to love of God. So we
remain in the darkness. If we walk in the light, then we are
enabled to acknowledge in joy and gratitude that everything good, beautiful, and true comes from God and is
offered to us in love.

Prayer

O God, you are not far from any of us,
since it is in you that we live,
and move, and exist.

You, who have overlooked the times of ignorance,
let everyone everywhere be told
that they must now repent.

— After Acts 17:27–28, 30

⚜ Friday after Ash Wednesday ⚜

For I am certain of this: neither death nor life, nor angels, nor principalities, nothing already in existence and nothing still to come, nor any power, nor the heights nor the depths, nor any created thing whatever, will be able to come between us and the love of God, known to us in Christ Jesus our Lord.

—Rom. 8:38–39

The love of God [has] become visible in Jesus. How is that love made visible through Jesus? It is made visible in the descending way. That is the great mystery of the Incarnation. God has descended to us human beings to become a human being with us; and once among us, descended to the total dereliction of one condemned to death. It isn't easy really to feel and understand from the inside this descending way of Jesus. Every fiber of our being rebels against it. We don't mind paying attention to poor people from time to time; but descending to a state of poverty and becoming poor with the poor, that we don't want to do. And yet that is the way Jesus chose as the way to know God....

God's way can only be grasped in prayer. The more you listen to God speaking within you, the sooner you will hear that voice inviting you to follow the way of Jesus. For Jesus' way is God's way and God's way is not for Jesus only but for everyone who is truly seeking God. Here we come up against the hard truth that the descending way of Jesus is also the way for us to find God. Jesus doesn't hesitate for a moment to make that clear.

The mystery of God's presence, therefore, can be touched only by a deep awareness of his absence. It is in the center of our longing for the absent God that we discover his footprints, and realize that our desire to love God is born out of the love with which he has touched us. In the patient waiting for the loved one, we discover how much he has filled our lives already. Just as the love of a mother for her son can grow deeper when he is far away, just as children can learn to appreciate their parents more when they have left the home, just as lovers can rediscover each other during long periods of absence, so our intimate relationship with God can become deeper and more mature by the purifying experience of his absence. By listening to our longings, we hear God as their creator. By touching the center of our solitude, we sense that we have been touched by loving hands. By watching carefully our endless desire to love, we come to the growing awareness that we can love only because we have been loved first, and that we can offer intimacy only because we are born out of the inner intimacy of God himself.

In our violent times, in which destruction of life is so rampant and the raw wounds of humanity so visible, it is very hard to tolerate the experience of God as a purifying absence, and to keep our hearts open so as to patiently and reverently prepare his way. We are tempted to grasp rapid solutions instead of inquiring about the validity of the questions. Our inclination to put faith in any suggestion that promises quick healing is so great that it is not surprising that spiritual experiences are mushrooming all over the place and have become highly sought after commercial items. Many people flock to places and persons who promise intensive experiences of togetherness, cathartic emotions of exhilaration and sweetness, and liberating sensations of rapture and ecstasy. In our desperate need for fulfillment and our restless search for the experience of divine intimacy, we are all too prone to construct our own spiritual events. In our impatient culture, it has indeed become extremely difficult to see much salvation in waiting.

But still ... the God who saves is not made by human hands. He transcends our psychological distinctions between "already" and "not yet," absence and presence, leaving and returning. Only in a patient waiting in expectation can we slowly break away from our illusions and pray as the psalmist prayed.

Prayer

God, you are my God, I am seeking you,
my soul is thirsting for you,
my flesh is longing for you,
a land parched, weary and waterless.
I long to gaze on you in the Sanctuary,
and to see your power and glory.

Your love is better than life itself,
my lips will recite your praise;
all my life I will bless you,
in your name lift up my hands;
my soul will feast most richly,
on my lips a song of joy and, in my mouth, praise.

On my bed I think of you,
I meditate on you all night long,
for you have always helped me.
I sing for joy in the shadow of your wings;
my soul clings close to you,
your right hand supports me.

—Ps. 63:1–8

❧ Saturday after Ash Wednesday ❧

When he went out after this, he noticed a tax collector, Levi by name, sitting at the tax office, and said to him, "Follow me." And leaving everything Levi got up and followed him.

—Luke 5:27–28

✠

Our lives are destined to become like the life of Jesus. The whole purpose of Jesus' ministry is to bring us to the house of his Father. Not only did Jesus come to free us from the bonds of sin and death, he also came to lead us into the intimacy of his divine life. It is difficult for us to imagine what this means. We tend to emphasize the distance between Jesus and ourselves. We see Jesus as the all-knowing and all-powerful Son of God who is unreachable for us sinful, broken human beings. But in thinking this way, we forget that Jesus came to give us his own life. He came to lift us up into loving community with the Father. Only when we recognize the radical purpose of Jesus' ministry will we be able to understand the meaning of the spiritual life. Everything that belongs to Jesus is given for us to receive.

✠

"Being in the world without being of the world." These words summarize well the way Jesus speaks of the spiritual life. It is a life in which we are totally transformed by the Spirit of love. Yet it is a life in which everything seems to remain the same. To live a spiritual life does not mean that we must leave our families, give up our jobs, or change our ways of working; it does not mean that we have to withdraw from social or political activities, or lose interest in literature and art; it does not require severe forms of asceticism or long hours of prayer. Changes such as these may in fact grow out of our spiritual life, and for some people radical decisions may be necessary. But the spiritual life can be lived in as many ways as there are people. What is new is that we have moved from the many things to the kingdom of God. What is new is that we are set free from the compulsions of our world and have set our hearts on the only necessary thing. What is new is that we no longer experience the many things, people, and events as endless causes for worry, but begin to experience them as the rich variety of ways in which God makes his presence known to us.

Prayer

> Lord, whoever serves you,
> must follow you,
> and your servant will be with you
> wherever you are.
> If anyone serves you,
> your Father will honor him.
> — After John 12:26

❧ First Sunday in Lent ❧

*The Lord your God is the one to whom you must do homage,
him alone you must serve.*

—Matt. 4:10

✠

Jesus' primary concern was to be obedient to his Father,
to live constantly in his presence. Only then did it become
clear to him what his task was in his relationships with
people. This also is the way he proposes for his apostles:
"It is to the glory of my Father that you should bear much
fruit and then you will be my disciples" (John 15:8). Perhaps we must continually remind ourselves that the first
commandment requiring us to love God with all our heart,
all our soul, and all our mind is indeed the first. I wonder if
we really believe this. It seems that in fact we live as if we
should give as much of our heart, soul, and mind as possible to our fellow human beings, while trying hard not to
forget God. At least we feel that our attention should be
divided evenly between God and our neighbor. But Jesus'
claim is much more radical. He asks for a single-minded
commitment to God and God alone. God wants all of our
heart, all of our mind, and all of our soul. It is this unconditional and unreserved love for God that leads to the
care for our neighbor, not as an activity which distracts
us from God or competes with our attention to God, but
as an expression of our love for God who reveals himself
to us as the God of all people. It is in God that we find
our neighbors and discover our responsibility to them. We
might even say that only in God does our neighbor become a neighbor rather than an infringement upon our

autonomy, and that only in and through God does service become possible.

✠

Still, I know that true joy comes from letting God love me the way God wants, whether it is through illness or health, failure or success, poverty or wealth, rejection or praise. It is hard for me to say, "I shall gratefully accept everything, Lord, that pleases you. Let your will be done." But I know that when I truly believe my Father is pure love, it will become increasingly possible to say these words from the heart.

Charles de Foucauld once wrote a prayer of abandonment that expresses beautifully the spiritual attitude I wish I had. . . .

It seems good to pray this prayer often. These are the words of a holy man, and they show the way I must go. I realize that I can never make this prayer come true by my own efforts. But the spirit of Jesus given to me can help me pray it and grow to its fulfillment. I know that my inner peace depends on my willingness to make this prayer my own.

Prayer

Father,
I abandon myself into your hands;
do with me what you will.
Whatever you may do, I thank you;
I am ready for all, I accept all.
Let only your will be done in me,
and in all your creatures.

I wish no more than this,
O Lord.

Into your hands I commend my soul;
I offer it to you with all the love
of my heart,
for I love you, Lord,
and so need to give myself,
to surrender myself into your hands,
without reserve
and with boundless confidence.
For you are my Father.

—Charles de Foucauld

⊰⊱ Monday of the First Week in Lent ⊰⊱

Then the King will say to those on his right hand, "Come, you whom my Father has blessed, take as your heritage the kingdom prepared for you since the foundation of the world. For I was hungry and you gave me food, I was thirsty and you gave me drink, I was a stranger and you made me welcome. . . . In truth I tell you, in so far as you did this to one of the least of these brothers of mine, you did it to me."

—Matt. 25:34–35, 40

✠

At first the word "hospitality" might evoke the image of soft sweet kindness, tea parties, bland conversations, and a general atmosphere of coziness. Probably this has its good reasons since in our culture the concept of hospitality has lost much of its power and is often used in circles where we are more prone to expect a watered down piety than a serious search for an authentic Christian spirituality. But still, if there is any concept worth restoring to its original depth and evocative potential, it is the concept of hospitality. It is one of the richest biblical terms that can deepen and broaden our insight in our relationships to our fellow human beings. Old and New Testament stories not only show how serious our obligation is to welcome the stranger in our home, but they also tell us that guests are carrying precious gifts with them, which they are eager to reveal to a receptive host. When Abraham received three strangers at Mamre and offered them water, bread, and a fine tender calf, they revealed themselves to him as the Lord announcing that Sarah his wife would give birth to a son (Gen. 18:1–15). When the widow of Zarephath offered food and shelter to Elijah, he revealed himself as a man of

God offering her an abundance of oil and meal and raising
her son from the dead (1 Kings 17:9–24). When the two
travelers to Emmaus invited the stranger, who had joined
them on the road to stay with them for the night, he made
himself known in the breaking of the bread as their Lord
and Savior (Luke 24:13–35).

When hostility is converted into hospitality then fearful
strangers can become guests revealing to their hosts the
promise they are carrying with them. Then, in fact, the
distinction between host and guest proves to be artificial
and evaporates in the recognition of the new-found unity.
Thus the biblical stories help us to realize not just that
hospitality is an important virtue, but even more that in
the context of hospitality guest and host can reveal their
most precious gifts and bring new life to each other.

✠

It remains true that loneliness often leads to hostile behavior and that solitude is the climate of hospitality. When we
feel lonely we have such a need to be liked and loved that
we are hypersensitive to the many signals in our environ-
ment and easily become hostile toward anyone whom we
perceive as rejecting us. But once we have found the center
of our life in our own heart and have accepted our alone-
ness, not as a fate but as a vocation, we are able to offer
freedom to others. Once we have given up our desire to
be fully fulfilled, we can offer emptiness to others. Once
we have become poor, we can be a good host. It is indeed
the paradox of hospitality that poverty makes a good host.
Poverty is the inner disposition that allows us to take away
our defenses and convert our enemies into friends. We can
only perceive the stranger as an enemy as long as we have
something to defend. But when we say, "Please enter —
my house is your house, my joy is your joy, my sadness is
your sadness, and my life is your life," we have nothing to
defend, since we have nothing to lose but all to give.

Turning the other cheek means showing our enemies that they can only be our enemies while supposing that we are anxiously clinging to our private property, whatever it is: our knowledge, our good name, our land, our money, or the many objects we have collected around us. But who will be our robber when everything he wants to steal from us becomes our gift to him? Who can lie to us, when only the truth will serve him well? Who wants to sneak into our back door, when our front door is wide open?

Poverty makes a good host. This paradoxical statement needs some more explanation. In order to be able to reach out to the other in freedom, two forms of poverty are very important, the poverty of mind and the poverty of heart.

Prayer

Dear Lord,
show me your kindness and your gentleness,
you who are meek and humble of heart.
So often I say to myself, "The Lord loves me,"
but very often this truth does not enter
into the center of my heart.

Let these weeks become an opportunity for me
to let go of all my resistances to your love
and an occasion for you to call me closer to you.
Amen.

⸙ Tuesday of the First Week in Lent ⸙

In your prayers do not babble as the gentiles do, for they think that by using many words they will make themselves heard. Do not be like them; your Father knows what you need before you ask him.

— Matt. 6:7–8

✠

For many of us prayer means nothing more than speaking with God. And since it usually seems to be a quite one-sided affair, prayer simply means talking to God. This idea is enough to create great frustrations. If I present a problem, I expect a solution; if I formulate a question, I expect an answer; if I ask for guidance, I expect a response. And when it seems, increasingly, that I am talking into the dark, it is not so strange that I soon begin to suspect that my dialogue with God is in fact a monologue. Then I may begin to ask myself: To whom am I really speaking, God or myself?...

The crisis of our prayer life is that our mind may be filled with ideas of God while our heart remains far from him.

✠

Finally, listen to your heart. It's there that Jesus speaks most intimately to you. Praying is first and foremost listening to Jesus, who dwells in the very depths of your heart. He doesn't shout. He doesn't thrust himself upon you. His voice is an unassuming voice, very nearly a whisper, the voice of a gentle love. Whatever you do with your life, go on listening to the voice of Jesus in your heart. This listening must be an active and very attentive listening, for in our restless and noisy world God's so loving voice is easily drowned out. You need to set aside some time every day

28

for this active listening to God if only for ten minutes. Ten minutes each day for Jesus alone can bring about a radical change in your life.

You'll find that it isn't easy to be still for ten minutes at a time. You'll discover straightaway that many other voices, voices that are very noisy and distracting, voices which do not come from God, demand your attention. But if you stick to your daily prayer time, then slowly but surely you'll come to hear the gentle voice of love and will long more and more to listen to it.

✠

Deep silence leads us to suspect that, in the first place, prayer is acceptance. A man who prays is a man standing with his hands open to the world. He knows that God will show himself in the nature which surrounds him, in the people he meets, in the situations he runs into. He trusts that the world holds God's secret within it, and he expects that secret to be shown to him. Prayer creates that openness where God can give himself to man. Indeed, God wants to give himself; he wants to surrender himself to the man he has created, he even begs to be admitted into the human heart.

Prayer

Why, O Lord, is it so hard for me
to keep my heart directed toward you?
Why does my mind wander off in so many directions,
and why does my heart desire
the things that lead me astray?
Let me sense your presence in the midst of my turmoil.
Take my tired body,
my confused mind,
and my restless soul into your arms
and give me rest, simple quiet rest.

So work out your salvation in fear and trembling. It is God who, for his own generous purpose, gives you the intention and the powers to act. Let your behavior be free of murmuring and complaining so that you remain faultless and pure unspoilt children of God.

— Phil. 2:12–15

God exists. When I can say this with all that I am, I have the "gnosis" (the knowledge of God) about which St. John speaks and the "Memoria Dei" (the memory of God) about which St. Basil writes. To say with all that we have, think, feel, and are: "God exists," is the most world-shattering statement that a human being can make. When we make that statement, all the distinctions between intellectual, emotional, affective, and spiritual understanding fall away and there is only one truth left to acclaim: God exists. When we say this from the heart, everything trembles in heaven and on earth. Because when God exists, all that is flows from him. When I want to know if I ever have come to the true knowledge, the gnosis, of God's existence, I have simply to allow myself to become aware of how I experience myself.... I am aware of my desire for food and clothing and shelter.... I am aware of my intellectual, physical, and artistic skills and my drive to use them. I am aware of my anger, my lust, my feelings of revenge and resentment, and even at times of my desire to harm. Indeed, what is central to me is: *I exist.* My own existence fills me, and wherever I turn I find myself again locked in my own self-awareness: I exist. Although experiences of hatred are different from experiences of love, and although a desire for power is different from a desire to serve, they all are the same insofar as they identify *my* existence as what *really* counts.

However, as soon as I say, "God exists," my existence no longer can remain in the center, because the essence of the knowledge of God reveals my own existence as deriving its total being from his. That is the true conversion experience. I no longer let the knowledge of my existence be the center from which I derive, project, deduct, or intuit the existence of God; I suddenly or slowly find my own existence revealed to me in and through the knowledge of God. Then it becomes real for me that I can love myself and my neighbor only because God has loved me first. The life-converting experience is not the discovery that I have choices to make that determine the way I live out my existence, but the awareness that my existence itself is not in the center. Once I "know" God, that is, once I experience his love as the love in which all my human experiences are anchored, I can only desire one thing: to be in that love.

✠

The converted person does not say that nothing matters any more, but that everything that is happens in God and that he is the dwelling place where we come to know the true order of things. Instead of saying: "Nothing matters any more, since I know that God exists," the converted person says: "All is now clothed in divine light and therefore nothing can be unimportant." The converted person sees, hears, and understands with a divine eye, a divine ear, a divine heart. The converted person knows himself or herself and all the world in God. The converted person is where God is, and from that place everything matters: giving water, clothing the naked, working for a new world order, saying a prayer, smiling at a child, reading a book, and sleeping in peace. All has become different while all remains the same.

Prayer

You who live in the secret place of Elyon,
spend your nights in the shelter of Shaddai,
saying to Yahweh, "My refuge, my fortress,
my God in whom I trust!"

You who say, "Yahweh my refuge!"

No disaster can overtake you,
no plague come near your tent;
he has given his angels orders about you
to guard you wherever you go.

—Ps. 91:1–2, 9, 10–11

✠ Thursday of the First Week in Lent ✠

Do not lose your fearlessness now, then, since the reward is so great. You will need perseverance if you are to do God's will and gain what he has promised.

— Heb. 10:35–36

Everything we know about Jesus indicates that he was concerned with only one thing: to do the will of his Father. Nothing in the Gospels is as impressive as Jesus' single-minded obedience to his Father. From his first recorded words in the Temple, "Did you not know that I must be busy with my Father's affairs?" (Luke 2:49), to his last words on the cross, "Father, into your hands I commit my spirit" (Luke 23:46), Jesus' only concern was to do the will of his Father. He says, "The Son can do nothing by himself; he can do only what he sees the Father doing" (John 5:19). The works Jesus did are the works the Father sent him to do, and the words he spoke are the words the Father gave him. He leaves no doubt about this: "If I am not doing my Father's work, there is no need to believe me ... " (John 10:37); "My word is not my own; it is the word of the one who sent me" (John 14:24).

Jesus is not our Savior simply because of what he said to us or did for us. He is our Savior because what he said and did was said and done in obedience to his Father. That is why St. Paul could say, "As by one man's disobedience many were made sinners, so by one man's obedience many will be made righteous" (Rom. 5:19). Jesus is the obedient one. The center of his life is this obedient relationship with the Father.

✠

Our lives are destined to become like the life of Jesus. The whole purpose of Jesus' ministry is to bring us to the house of his Father. Not only did Jesus come to free us from the bonds of sin and death, he also came to lead us into the intimacy of his divine life. It is difficult for us to imagine what this means. We tend to emphasize the distance between Jesus and ourselves. We see Jesus as the all-knowing and all-powerful Son of God who is unreachable for us sinful, broken human beings. But in thinking this way, we forget that Jesus came to give us his own life. He came to lift us up into loving community with the Father. Only when we recognize the radical purpose of Jesus' ministry will we be able to understand the meaning of the spiritual life. Everything that belongs to Jesus is given for us to receive. All that Jesus does we may also do.

Prayer

God, create in me a clean heart,
renew within me a resolute spirit,
do not thrust me away from your presence,
do not take away from me your spirit of holiness.

—Ps. 51:10–11

So then, if you are bringing your offering to the altar and there remember that your brother has something against you, leave your offering there before the altar, go and be reconciled with your brother first, and then come back and present your offering. Come to terms with your opponent in good time while you are still on the way to the court with him.

— Matt. 5:23–25

✠

This morning I meditated on God's eagerness to forgive me, revealed in the words of Psalm 103: "As the distance of east from west, so far from us does he put our faults." In the midst of all my distractions, I was touched by God's desire to forgive me again and again. If I return to God with a repentant heart after I have sinned, God is always there to embrace me and let me start afresh. "The Lord is compassion and love, slow to anger and rich in mercy."

It is hard for me to forgive someone who has really offended me, especially when it happens more than once. I begin to doubt the sincerity of the one who asks forgiveness for a second, third, or fourth time. But God does not keep count. God just waits for our return, without resentment or desire for revenge. God wants us home. "The love of the Lord is everlasting."

Maybe the reason it seems hard for me to forgive others is that I do not fully believe that I am a forgiven person. If I could fully accept the truth that I am forgiven and do not have to live in guilt or shame, I would really be free. My freedom would allow me to forgive others seventy times seven times. By not forgiving, I chain myself to a desire to get even, thereby losing my freedom. A forgiven person forgives. This is what we proclaim when we pray, "and forgive us our trespasses as we forgive those who have trespassed against us."

This lifelong struggle lies at the heart of the Christian life.

✠

The love of God is an unconditional love, and only that love can empower us to live together without violence. When we know that God loves us deeply and will always go on loving us, whoever we are and whatever we do, it becomes possible to expect no more of our fellow men and women than they are able to give, to forgive them generously when they have offended us, and always to respond to their hostility with love. By doing so we make visible a new way of being human and a new way of responding to our world problems.

Prayer

Bless Yahweh, my soul.
never forget all his acts of kindness.

He does not treat us as our sins deserve,
nor repay us as befits our offenses.

As the height of heaven above earth,
so strong is his faithful love for those who fear him.
As the distance of east from west,
so far from us does he put our faults.

As tenderly as a father treats his children,
so Yahweh treats those who fear him.

—Ps. 103:2, 10–13

❖❄ Saturday of the First Week in Lent ❄❖

I say this to you, love your enemies and pray for those who persecute you; so that you may be children of your Father in heaven, for he causes his sun to rise on the bad as well as the good, and sends down rain to fall on the upright and the wicked alike.

—Matt. 5:44–45

✠

Christians mention one another in their prayers (Rom. 1:9, 2 Cor. 1:11, Eph. 6:8, Col. 4:3), and in so doing they bring help and even salvation to those for whom they pray (Rom. 15:30, Phil. 1:19). But the final test of compassionate prayer goes beyond prayers for fellow Christians, members of the community, friends, and relatives. Jesus says it most unambiguously, "I say this to you: love your enemies and pray for those who persecute you" (Matt. 5:44); and in the depth of his agony on the cross, he prays for those who are killing him, "Father, forgive them; they do not know what they are doing" (Luke 23:34). Here the full significance of the discipline of prayer becomes visible. Prayer allows us to lead into the center of our hearts not only those who love us but also those who hate us. This is possible only when we are willing to make our enemies part of ourselves and thus convert them first of all in our own hearts.

The first thing we are called to do when we think of others as our enemies is to pray for them. This is certainly not easy. It requires discipline to allow those who hate us or those toward whom we have hostile feelings to come into the intimate center of our hearts. People who make our lives difficult and cause us frustration, pain, or even harm

37

are least likely to receive a place in our hearts. Yet every time we overcome this impatience with our opponents and are willing to listen to the cry of those who persecute us, we will recognize them as brothers and sisters too. Praying for our enemies is therefore a real event, the event of reconciliation. It is impossible to lift our enemies up in the presence of God and at the same time continue to hate them. Seen in the place of prayer, even the unprincipled dictator and the vicious torturer can no longer appear as the object of fear, hatred, and revenge, because when we pray we stand at the center of the great mystery of Divine Compassion. Prayer converts the enemy into a friend and is thus the beginning of a new relationship. There is probably no prayer as powerful as the prayer for our enemies. But it is also the most difficult prayer since it is most contrary to our impulses. This explains why some saints consider prayer for our enemies the main criterion of holiness.

Love your enemies, do good to those who hate you, bless those who curse you, pray for those who treat you badly....

These sayings express not only the essence of nonviolent resistance, but also the heart of Jesus' preaching. If anyone should ask you what are the most radical words in the Gospel, you need not hesitate to reply: "Love your enemies." It's these words that reveal to us most clearly the kind of love proclaimed by Jesus. In these words we have the clearest expression of what it means to be a disciple of Jesus. Love for one's enemy is the touchstone of being a Christian.

Prayer

O Lord, look with favor on us, your people,
and impart your love to us —
not as an idea or concept, but as a lived experience.
We can love each other
only because you have loved us first.
Let us know that first love
so that we can see all human love
as a reflection of a greater love,
a love without conditions and limitations.
Amen.

❦ Second Sunday in Lent ❧

He was still speaking when suddenly a bright cloud covered them with shadow, and suddenly from the cloud there came a voice which said, "This is my Son, the Beloved; he enjoys my favor. Listen to him."

— Matt. 17:5

✠

When we break bread together, we reveal to each other the real story of Christ's life and our lives in him. Jesus took bread, blessed it, broke it, and gave it to this friends. He did so when he saw a hungry crowd and felt compassion for them (Matt. 14:19; 15:36); he did it on the evening before his death when he wanted to say farewell (Matt. 26:26); he did so when he made himself known to the two disciples whom he met on the road to Emmaus (Luke 24:30). And ever since his death, Christians have done so in memory of him.

Thus, the breaking of the bread is the celebration, the making present, of Christ's story as well as our own. In the taking, blessing, breaking, and giving of the bread, the mystery of Christ's life is expressed in the most succinct way. The Father took his only Son and sent him into the world so that through him the world might be saved (John 3:17). At the river Jordan and on Mount Tabor he blessed him with the words, "This is my Son, the Beloved, my favor rests on him...listen to him" (Matt. 3:17, 17:5). The blessed one was broken on a cross, "pierced through for our faults, crushed for our sins" (Isa. 53:5). But through his death he gave himself to us as our food, thus fulfilling the words he spoke to his disciples at the last supper, "This is my body which will be given for you" (Luke 22:19).

40

It is in this life that is taken, blessed, broken, and given that Jesus Christ wants to make us participants. Therefore, while breaking bread with his disciples, he said, "Do this as a memorial of me" (Luke 22:19). When we eat bread and drink wine together in memory of Christ, we become intimately related to his own compassionate life. In fact, we *become* his life and are thus enabled to represent his life in our time and place.

✠

That is the great mystery of the Incarnation. God has descended to us human beings to become a human being with us; and once among us, descended to the total dereliction of one condemned to death.... In the first century of Christianity there was already a hymn being sung about this descending way of Jesus. Paul puts it into his Letter to the Philippians in order to commend to his people the descending direction on the ladder of life. He writes:

> Make your own the mind of Christ Jesus:
> Who, being in the form of God,
> did not count equality with God
> something to be grasped.
> But he emptied himself,
> taking the form of a slave,
> becoming as human beings are;
> and being in every way like a human being,
> he was humbler yet,
> even to accepting death, death on a cross.

Here, expressed in summary but very plain terms, is the way of God's love. It is a way that goes down further and further into the greatest destitution: the destitution of a criminal whose life is taken from him.

✠

Jesus loves his disciples with the same love that the Father loves him, and as this love makes Jesus one with the Father, so too does it make the disciples one with Jesus.

Prayer

God, you have told us
to listen to your beloved Son.
Nourish us with your word
and cleanse the eyes of our spirit,
so that we may know your glory.
We ask this through Jesus Christ.

⊰⊱ Monday of the Second Week in Lent ⊰⊱

Be compassionate just as your Father is compassionate. Do not judge, and you will not be judged: do not condemn and you will not be condemned; forgive, and you will be forgiven.

—Luke 6:36–37

✠

Jesus' command, "Be compassionate as your Father is compassionate," is a command to participate in the compassion of God himself. He requires us to unmask the illusion of our competitive selfhood, to give up clinging to our imaginary distinctions as sources of identity, and to be taken up into the same intimacy with God which he himself knows. This is the mystery of the Christian life: to receive a new self, a new identity, which depends not on what we can achieve, but on what we are willing to receive. This new self is our participation in the divine life in and through Christ. Jesus wants us to belong to God as he belongs to God; he wants us to be children of God as he is a child of God; he wants us to let go of the old life, which is so full of fears and doubts, and to receive the new life, the life of God himself. In and through Christ we receive a new identity that enables us to say, "I am not the esteem I can collect through competition, but the love I have freely received from God." It allows us to say with Paul, "I live now not with my own life but with the life of Christ who lives in me" (Gal. 2:20).

This new self, the self of Jesus Christ, makes it possible for us to be compassionate as our Father is compassionate. Through union with him, we are lifted out of our competitiveness with each other into the divine wholeness. By sharing in the wholeness of the one in whom no

43

competition exists, we can enter into new, compassionate relationships with each other. By accepting our identities from the one who is the giver of all life, we can be with each other without distance or fear. This new identity, free from greed and desire for power, allows us to enter so fully and unconditionally into the sufferings of others that it becomes possible for us to heal the sick and call the dead to life. When we share in God's compassion, a whole new way of living opens itself to us, a way of living we glimpse in the lives of the Apostles and those great Christians who have witnessed for Christ through the centuries. This divine compassion is not, like our self-made compassion, part of the competition. Rather, it is the expression of a new way of living in which interpersonal comparisons, rivalries, and competitions are gradually left behind.

✠

Compassion asks us to go where it hurts, to enter into places of pain, to share in brokenness, fear, confusion, and anguish. Compassion challenges us to cry out with those in misery, to mourn with those who are lonely, to weep with those in tears. Compassion requires us to be weak with the weak, vulnerable with the vulnerable, and powerless with the powerless. Compassion means full immersion in the condition of being human. . . . It is not surprising that compassion, understood as suffering with, often evokes in us a deep resistance and even protest. We are inclined to say, "This is self-flagellation, this is masochism, this is a morbid interest in pain, this is a sick desire." It is important for us to acknowledge this resistance and to recognize that suffering is not something we desire or to which we are attracted. On the contrary, it is something we want to avoid at all cost. Therefore, compassion is not among our most natural responses. We are pain-avoiders and we consider anyone who feels attracted to suffering abnormal, or at least very unusual.

Prayer

O Lord Jesus,
you who came to us
to show the compassionate love of your Father,
make your people know this love
with their hearts, minds, and souls.

And to me, O Lord, your stumbling friend,
show your mercy.
Amen.

The greatest among you must be your servant. Anyone who raises himself up will be humbled, and anyone who humbles himself will be raised up.

—Matt. 23:11–12

✠

[Jesus invites us] to follow him on his humbling way: "The one who humbles himself will be exalted" (Luke 14:11). "Anyone who loses his life for my sake, and for the sake of the gospel, will save it" (Mark 8:35). "The one who makes himself as little as this little child is the greatest in the kingdom of heaven" (Matt. 18:4). "If anyone wants to be a follower of mine, let him renounce himself and take up his cross and follow me" (Mark 8:34). "How happy are the poor in spirit . . . those who mourn . . . those who hunger . . . who are persecuted" (Matt. 5:3–10). "Love your enemies and pray for those who persecute you" (Matt. 5:44).

This is the way of Jesus and the way to which he calls his disciples. It is the way that at first frightens or at least embarrasses us. Who wants to be humble? Who wants to be the last? Who wants to be like a little, powerless child? Who desires to lose his or her life, to be poor, mourning, and hungry? All this appears to be against our natural inclinations. But once we see that Jesus reveals to us, in his radically downward pull, the compassionate nature of God, we begin to understand that to follow him is to participate in the ongoing self-revelation of God.

✠

[Jesus] presents to us the great mystery of the descending way. It is the way of suffering, but also the way to heal-

46

ing. It is the way of humiliation, but also the way to the resurrection. It is the way of tears, but of tears that turn into tears of joy. It is the way of hiddenness, but also the way that leads to the light that will shine for all people. It is the way of persecution, oppression, martyrdom, and death, but also the way to the full disclosure of God's love. In the Gospel of John, Jesus says: "As Moses lifted up the snake in the desert, so must the Son of man be lifted up." You see in these words how the descending way of Jesus becomes the ascending way. The "lifting up" that Jesus speaks of refers both to his being raised up on the cross in total humiliation and to his being raised up from the dead in total glorification. . . .

You are probably wondering how, in imitation of Jesus, you are to find that descending way. That's a very personal and intimate question, and in the end I don't think that anyone can answer it but you. It's not simply a matter of renouncing your money, your possessions, your intellectual formation, or your friends or family. For some people, it has indeed meant this but only because they felt personally called to take that road. Each one of us has to seek out his or her own descending way of love. That calls for much prayer, much patience, and much guidance. It has nothing at all to do with spiritual heroics, dramatically throwing everything overboard to "follow" Jesus. The descending way is a way that is concealed in each person's heart. But because it is so seldom walked on, it's often overgrown with weeds. Slowly but surely we have to clear the weeds, open the way, and set out on it unafraid.

For me, this weeding out process is always related to prayer, because to pray is to make free time for God, even when you're very busy with important matters of one kind or another. Every time you make free time for God, you clear up a bit of the descending path, and you see where you can plant your feet on the way of love.

Prayer

Lord Jesus Christ, make ours
the same attitude that was yours.
You who emptied yourself,
taking the form of a slave,
you humbled yourself,
becoming obedient to death,
even death on a cross.

— After Phil. 2:5, 7–8

⚜ Wednesday of the Second Week in Lent ⚜

Anyone who wants to become great among you must be your servant and anyone who wants to be first among you must be your slave, just as the Son of man came not to be served but to serve, and to give his life as a ransom for many.

— Matt. 20:26–28

✠

The great mystery of God's compassion is that in his compassion, in his entering with us into the condition of a slave, he reveals himself to us as God. His becoming a servant is not an exception to his being God. His self-emptying and humiliation are not a step away from his true nature. His becoming as we are and dying on a cross is not a temporary interruption of his of divine existence. Rather, in the emptied and humbled Christ we encounter God, we see who God really is, we come to know his true divinity.

In his servanthood God does not disfigure himself, he does not take on something alien to himself, he does not act against or in spite of his divine self. On the contrary, it is in his servanthood that God chooses to reveal himself as God to us. Therefore, we can say that the downward pull as we see this in Jesus Christ is not a movement away from God, but a movement toward him as he really is: A God for us who came not to rule but to serve. This implies very specifically that God does not want to be known except through servanthood and that, therefore, servanthood is God's self-revelation.

✠

Radical servanthood does not make sense unless we introduce a new level of understanding and see it as the

way to encounter God himself. To be humble and persecuted cannot be desired unless we can find God in
humility and persecution. When we begin to see God
himself, the source of all our comfort and consolation,
in the center of servanthood, compassion becomes much
more than doing good for unfortunate people. Radical
servanthood, as the encounter with the compassionate
God, takes us beyond the distinctions between wealth
and poverty, success and failure, fortune and bad luck.
Radical servanthood is not an enterprise in which we try
to surround ourselves with as much misery as possible,
but a joyful way of life in which our eyes are opened
to the vision of the true God who chose the way of servanthood to make himself known. The poor are called
blessed not because poverty is good, but because theirs
is the kingdom of heaven; the mourners are called blessed
not because mourning is good, but because they shall
be comforted.

Here we are touching the profound spiritual truth that
service is an expression of the search for God and not just
of the desire to bring about individual or social change.

✠

Joy and gratitude are the qualities of the heart by which we
recognize those who are committed to a life of service in
the path of Jesus Christ.... Wherever we see real service
we also see joy, because in the midst of service a divine
presence becomes visible and a gift is offered. Therefore,
those who serve as followers of Jesus discover that they are
receiving more than they are giving. Just as a mother does
not need to be rewarded for the attention she pays to her
child, because her child is her joy, so those who serve their
neighbor will find their reward in the people whom they
serve. The joy of those who follow their Lord on his self-
emptying and humbling way shows that what they seek is
not misery and pain but the God whose compassion they

have felt in their own lives: Their eyes do not focus on poverty and misery, but on the face of the loving.

Prayer

Lord,
you are the Way, the Truth, and the Life.
No one comes to the Father
except through you.

— After John 14:6

❧ Thursday of the Second Week in Lent ❧

I, Yahweh, search the heart,
test the motives,
to give each person what his conduct
and his actions deserve.

—Jer. 17:10

✠

It is not so difficult to see that, in our particular world, we all have a strong desire to accomplish something. Some of us think in terms of great dramatic changes in the structure of our society. Others want at least to build a house, write a book, invent a machine, or win a trophy. And some of us seem to be content when we just do something worthwhile for someone. But practically all of us think about ourselves in terms of our contribution to life. And when we have become old, much of our feelings of happiness or sadness depends on our evaluation of the part we played in giving shape to our world and its history....

When we start being too impressed by the results of our work, we slowly come to the erroneous conviction that life is one large scoreboard where someone is listing the points to measure our worth. And before we are fully aware of it, we have sold our soul to the many grade-givers. That means we are not only in the world, but also of the world. Then we become what the world makes us. We are intelligent because someone gives us a high grade. We are helpful because someone says thanks. We are likable because someone likes us. And we are important because someone considers us indispensable. In short, we are worthwhile because we have successes.

✠

To live a Christian life means to live *in* the world without being *of* it. It is in solitude that this inner freedom can grow....

A life without a lonely place, that is, a life without a quiet center, easily becomes destructive. When we cling to the results of our actions as our only way of self-identification, then we become possessive and defensive and tend to look at our fellow human beings more as enemies to be kept at a distance than as friends with whom we share the gifts of life.

In solitude we can slowly unmask the illusion of our possessiveness and discover in the center of our own self that we are not what we can conquer, but what is given to us. In solitude we can listen to the voice of him who spoke to us before we could speak a word, who healed us before we could make any gesture to help, who set us free long before we could free others, and who loved us long before we could give love to anyone. It is in this solitude that we discover that being is more important than having, and that we are worth more than the result of our efforts. In solitude we discover that our life is not a possession to be defended, but a gift to be shared. It's there we recognize that the healing words we speak are not just our own, but are given to us; that the love we can express is part of a greater love; and that the new life we bring forth is not a property to cling to, but a gift to be received.

In solitude we become aware that our worth is not the same as our usefulness.

Prayer

Yahweh, you examine me and know me,
you know when I sit, when I rise,
you understand my thoughts from afar.
You watch when I walk or lie down,
you know every detail of my conduct.

God, examine me and know my heart,
test me and know my concerns.
Make sure that I am not on my way to ruin,
and guide me on the road of eternity.

— Ps. 139:1–3, 23–24

❧ Friday of the Second Week in Lent ☙

*I tell you, then, that the kingdom of God will be taken from
you and given to a people who will produce its fruit.*

—Matt. 21:43

✠

Even though it may be realistic to admit that there is hardly
any news in the sermon for most people, the core message
of the Gospel nonetheless contains a Truth that no one has
yet fully made true. And real listening means nothing less
than the constant willingness to confess that you have not
yet realized what you profess to believe. Who likes to hear,
for example, that the last will be first, if he happens to be
first? And who wants to hear that those who are poor, who
mourn, who are hungry, thirsty, and persecuted are called
happy, when he is wealthy, self-content, well-fed, praised
for his good wines, and admired by all his friends? Who
wants to hear that he has to love his enemies and pray for
those who persecute him when he calls his boss an S.O.B.,
his own son a good-for-nothing tramp....

The message might be the same all through life and
might be repeated over and over again in different words
and styles, but he who will let it really come through allows
himself, at the same time, the possibility of coming to an
insight that might well have consequences for his style of
life, which he is not eager to take. The truth, after all, is
radical: It goes to the roots of a man's life in such a way
that few are those who want it and the freedom it brings
with it. There is, in fact, such an outright fear to face the
Truth in all its directness and simplicity the irritation and
anger seem to be a more common human response than

a humble confession that one also belongs to the group
Jesus criticized.

✠

For a Christian is only a Christian when he unceasingly
asks critical questions of the society in which he lives
and continuously stresses the necessity for conversion,
not only of the individual but also of the world. A Christian is only a Christian when he refuses to allow himself
or anyone else to settle into a comfortable rest. He remains dissatisfied with the *status quo*. And he believes
that he has an essential role to play in the realization of
the new world to come — even if he cannot say how
that world will come about. A Christian is only a Christian when he keeps saying to everyone he meets that the
good news of the Kingdom has to be proclaimed to the
whole world and witnessed to all nations (Matt. 24:13).
As long as a Christian lives he keeps searching for a new
order without divisions between people, for a new structure that allows every man to shake hands with every
other man, and a new life in which there will be lasting
unity and peace. He will not allow his neighbor to stop
moving, to lose courage, or to escape into small everyday
pleasures to which he can cling. He is irritated by satisfaction and self-content in himself as well as in others since
he knows, with an unshakable certainty, that something
great is coming of which he has already seen the first rays
of light. He believes that this world not only passes but
has to pass in order to let the new world be born. He
believes that there will never be a moment in this life in
which one can rest in the supposition that there is nothing left to do. But he will not despair when he does not
see the result he wanted to see. For in the midst of all
his work he keeps hearing the words of the One sitting
on the throne: "I am making the whole of creation new"
(Rev. 21:5).

Prayer

God, you wish to reveal to us
how rich is the glory of your mystery
among the gentiles;
it is Christ among us, our hope of glory!
This is the Christ
we are proclaiming, admonishing, and instructing
everyone in all wisdom,
to make everyone perfect in Christ.

— After Col. 1:7–28

✠ Saturday of the Second Week in Lent ✠

I will leave this place and go to my father and say: "Father, I have sinned against heaven and against you; I no longer deserve to be called your son; treat me as one of your hired men." So he left the place and went back to his father.

While he was still a long way off, his father saw him and was moved with pity. He ran to the boy, clasped him in his arms and kissed him.

—Luke 15:18–20

✠

[This] is a story about returning. I realize the importance of returning over and over again. My life drifts away from God. I have to return.... Returning is a lifelong struggle.

It strikes me that the wayward son had rather selfish motivations. He said to himself, "How many of my father's paid servants have more food than they want, and here am I dying of hunger! I will leave this place and go to my father." He didn't return because of a renewed love for his father. No, he returned simply to survive. He had discovered that the way he had chosen was leading him to death. Returning to his father was a necessity for staying alive. He realized that he had sinned, but this realization came about because sin had brought him close to death.

I am moved by the fact that the father didn't require any higher motivation. His love was so total and unconditional that he simply welcomed his son home.

This is a very encouraging thought. God does not require a pure heart before embracing us. Even if we return only because following our desires has failed to bring happiness, God will take us back. Even if we return because being a Christian brings us more peace than being a pagan,

God will receive us. Even if we return because our sins did not offer as much satisfaction as we had hoped, God will take us back. Even if we return because we could not make it on our own, God will receive us. God's love does not require any explanations about why we are returning. God is glad to see us home and wants to give us all we desire, just for being home.

In my mind's eye I see Rembrandt's painting *The Return of the Prodigal Son*. The dim-eyed old father holds his returned son close to his chest with an unconditional love.... He seems to think only one thing: "He is back home, and I am so glad to have him with me again."

✠

The voice of despair says, "I sin over and over again. After endless promises to myself and others to do better next time, I find myself back again in the old dark places. Forget about trying to change. I have tried for years. It didn't work and it will never work. It is better that I get out of people's way, be forgotten, no longer around, dead."

This strangely attractive voice takes all uncertainties away and puts an end to the struggle. It speaks unambiguously for the darkness and offers a clear-cut negative identity.

But Jesus came to open my ears to another voice that says, "I am your God, I have molded you with my own hands, and I love what I have made. I love you with a love that has no limits, because I love you as I am loved. Do not run away from me. Come back to me — not once, not twice, but always again. You are my child. How can you ever doubt that I will embrace you again, hold you against my breast, kiss you and let my hands run through your hair? I am your God — the God of mercy and compassion, the God of pardon and love, the God of tenderness and care. Please do not say that I have given up on you, that I cannot stand you any more, that there is no way back. It

is not true. I so much want you to be with me. I so much
want you to be close to me. I know all your thoughts. I
hear all your words. I see all of your actions. And I love
you because you are beautiful, made in my own image, an
expression of my most intimate love. Do not judge yourself. Do not condemn yourself. Do not reject yourself. Let
my love touch the deepest, most hidden corners of your
heart and reveal to you your own beauty, a beauty that
you have lost sight of, but which will become visible to
you again in the light of my mercy. Come, come, let me
wipe your tears, and let my mouth come close to your ear
and say to you, 'I love you, I love you, I love you.' "

This is the voice that Jesus wants us to hear. It is the
voice that calls us always to return to the one who has
created us in love and wants to re-create us in mercy.

Prayer

O Lord, my Lord,
help me to listen to your voice
and to decide for your mercy.

❧ Third Sunday in Lent ❧

Whoever drinks this water
will be thirsty again;
but no one who drinks the water that I shall give him
will ever be thirsty again:
the water that I shall give him
will become in him a spring of water, welling up for
  eternal life.

—John 4:14

✠

In the midst of Lent I am made aware that Easter is coming again: the days are becoming longer, the snow is withdrawing, the sun is bringing new warmth, and a bird is singing. Yesterday, during the night prayers, a cat was crying! Indeed, spring announces itself. And tonight, O Lord, I heard you speak to the Samaritan woman. You said: "Anyone who drinks the water that I shall give will never be thirsty again; the water that I shall give will turn into a spring inside him, welling up to eternal life." What words! They are worth many hours, days, and weeks of reflection. I will carry them with me in my preparation for Easter. The water that you give turns into a spring. Therefore, I do not have to be stingy with your gift, O Lord. I can freely let the water come from my center and let anyone who desires drink from it. Perhaps I will even see this spring in myself when others come to it to quench their thirst.

✠

In the Eucharist God's love is most concretely made present. Jesus has not only become human, he has also become bread and wine in order that, through our eating and our drinking, God's love might become our own. The great

mystery of the Eucharist is that God's love is offered to us
not in the abstract, but in a very concrete way; not as a
theory, but as food for our daily life. The Eucharist opens
the way for us to make God's love our own. Jesus himself
makes that clear to us when he says:

> ... my flesh is real food
> and my blood is real drink.
> Whoever eats my flesh and drinks my blood
> lives in me and I live in that person.
> As the living Father sent me
> and I draw life from the Father,
> so whoever eats me will also draw life from me.

Whenever you receive the body and blood of Jesus in the
Eucharist, his love is given to you, the same love that he
showed on the cross. It is the love of God for all people of
all times and places, all religions and creeds, all races and
classes, all tribes and nations, all sinners and saints.

On the cross, Jesus has shown us how far God's love
goes. It's a love which embraces even those who crucified him. When Jesus is hanging nailed to the cross, totally
broken and stripped of everything, he still prays for his ex-
ecutioners: "Father, forgive them; they do not know what
they are doing." Jesus' love for his enemies knows no
bounds. He prays even for those who are putting him to
death. It is this, the enemy-loving love of God, that is offered to us in the Eucharist. To forgive our enemies doesn't
lie within our power. That is a divine gift. That's why it's
so important to make the Eucharist the heart and center of
your life. It's there that you receive the love which empow-
ers you to take the way that Jesus has taken before you: a
narrow way, a painful way, but the way that gives you true
joy and peace and enables you to make the non-violent
love of God visible in this world.

Prayer

As a deer yearns
for running streams,
so I yearn
for you, my God.

In you is the source of life,
by your light we see the light.

—Ps. 42:1; 36:9

"In truth I tell you, no prophet is ever accepted in his own country."...

When they heard this everyone in the synagogue was enraged. They sprang to their feet and hustled him out of the town; and they took him up to the brow of the hill their town was built on, intending to throw him off the cliff, but he passed straight through the crowd and walked away.

— Luke 4:24, 28–30

✠

He became a human being among a small, oppressed people, under very difficult circumstances. He was held in contempt by the rulers of his country and was put to a shameful death between two criminals.

There was nothing spectacular about Jesus' life. Far from it! Even when you look at Jesus' miracles, you find that he did not heal or revive people in order to get publicity. He frequently forbade them even to talk about it. His resurrection too was a hidden event. Only his disciples and a few of the women and men who had known him intimately before his death saw him as the risen Lord.

Now that Christianity has become one of the major world religions and millions of people utter the name of Jesus every day, it's hard for us to believe that Jesus revealed God in hiddenness. But neither Jesus' life nor his death nor his resurrection were intended to astound us with the great power of God. God became a lowly, hidden, almost invisible God....

That's a mystery which is difficult to grasp in an age that attaches so much value to publicity. We tend to think that the more people know and talk about something, the more important it must be. That's understandable, considering the fact that great notoriety often means big money, and big money often means a large degree of power, and power easily creates the illusion of importance. In our society, it's often statistics that determine what's important: the best-selling LP, the most popular book, the richest man, the highest tower-block, the most expensive car.

✠

It strikes me again and again that, in our publicity-seeking world, a lot of discussions about God take it as their starting point that even God has to justify himself. People often say: "If that God of yours really exists, then why doesn't he make his omnipotence more visible in this chaotic world of ours?" God is called to account, as it were, and mockingly invited to prove, just for once, that he really does exist. Again, you often hear someone say: "I've no need whatever for God. I can perfectly well look after myself. As a matter of fact, I've yet to receive any help from God with my problems!" The bitterness and sarcasm evident in remarks of this sort show what's expected: that God should at least be concerned about his own popularity. People often talk as though God has as great a need for recognition as we do.

Now look at Jesus, who came to reveal God to us, and you see that popularity in any form is the very thing he avoids. He is constantly pointing out that God reveals himself in secrecy. It sounds very paradoxical, but accepting and, I would venture to say, entering into that paradox sets you on the road of the spiritual life.

Prayer

Lord, I pray for all who witness for you in this world:
ministers, priests, and bishops,
men and women who have dedicated their lives to you,
and all those who try to bring the light of the Gospel
into the darkness of this age.
Give them courage, strength, perseverance, and hope;
fill their hearts and minds
with the knowledge of your presence,
and let them experience your name
as their refuge from all dangers.
Most of all, give them the joy of your Spirit,
so that wherever they go and whomever they meet
they will remove the veil
of depression, fatalism, and defeatism
and will bring new life to the many
who live in constant fear of death.
Lord, be with all who bring the Good News.
Amen.

⁂ Tuesday of the Third Week in Lent ⁂

*Then the master sent for the man and said to him, "You wicked
servant, I cancelled all that debt of yours when you appealed
to me. Were you not bound, then, to have pity on your fellow-
servant just as I had pity on you?" And in his anger the master
handed him over to the torturers till he should pay all his debt.
And that is how my heavenly Father will deal with you unless
you each forgive your brother from your heart.*

—Matt. 18:32–35

✠

God's compassion is not something abstract or indefinite,
but a concrete, specific gesture in which God reaches out to
us. In Jesus Christ we see the fullness of God's compassion.
To us, who cry out from the depth of our brokenness for a
hand that will touch us, an arm that can embrace us, lips
that will kiss us, a word that speaks to us here and now,
and a heart that is not afraid of our fears and tremblings; to
us, who feel our own pain as no other human being feels
it, has felt it, or ever will feel it and who are always waiting
for someone who dares to come close — to us a man has
come who could truly say, "I am with you." Jesus Christ,
who is God-with-us, has come to us in the freedom of love,
not needing to experience our human condition.

✠

In Jesus Christ the obedient servant, who did not cling to
his divinity but emptied himself and became as we are,
God has revealed the fullness of his compassion. He is
Immanuel, God-with-us. The great call we have heard is
to live a compassionate life....

As long as we live on this earth, our lives as Christians
must be marked by compassion. But we must [realize] that

67

the compassionate life is not our final goal. In fact, we can only live the compassionate life to the fullest when we know that it points beyond itself. We know that he who emptied and humbled himself has been raised high and has been given a name above all other names, and we know too that he left us to prepare a place for us where suffering will be overcome and compassion no longer necessary. There is a new heaven and a new earth for which we hope with patient expectation. This is the vision presented in the Book of Revelation:

> Then I saw a new heaven and a new earth; the first heaven and the first earth had disappeared now, and there was no longer any sea. I saw the holy city, and the new Jerusalem, coming down from God out of heaven, as beautiful as a bride all dressed for her husband. Then I heard a loud voice call from the throne, "You see this city? Here God lives among men. He will make his home among them; they shall be his people, and he will be their God; his name is God-with-them. He will wipe away all tears from their eyes; there will be no more death, and no more mourning or sadness. The world of the past has gone."
>
> —Rev. 21:1–4

This is the vision that guides us. This vision makes us share one another's burdens, carry our crosses together, and unite for a better world. This vision takes the despair out of death and the morbidity out of suffering, and opens new horizons. This vision also gives us the energy to manifest its first realization in the midst of the complexities of life. This vision is indeed of a future world. But it is no utopia. The future has already begun and is revealed each time strangers are welcomed, the naked are clothed, the sick and prisoners are visited, and oppression is overcome.

Through these grateful actions the first glimpses of a new heaven and a new earth can be seen.

Prayer

Dear Lord, help me keep my eyes on you.
You are the incarnation of Divine Love,
you are the expression of God's infinite compassion,
you are the visible manifestation of the Father's holiness.
You are beauty, goodness, gentleness,
forgiveness, and mercy.

To you I want to give all that I am.
Let me be generous, not stingy or hesitant.

⚜ Wednesday of the Third Week in Lent ⚜

But take care, as you value your lives! Do not forget the things which you yourselves have seen, or let them slip from your heart as long as you live; teach them, rather, to your children and to your children's children.

—Deut. 4:9

✠

Indeed it is in memory that we enter into a nurturing and sustaining relationship with Christ. In his farewell discourse Jesus said to his disciples, "It is for your own good that I am going, because unless I go, the Advocate will not come to you; . . . But when the Spirit of truth comes he will lead you to the complete truth" (John 16:7, 13). Here Jesus reveals to his closest friends that only in memory will real intimacy with him be possible, that only in memory will they experience the full meaning of what they have witnessed.

They listened to his words, they saw him on Mount Tabor, they heard him speak about his death and resurrection, but their ears and eyes remained closed and they did not understand. The Spirit, his spirit, had not yet come, and although they saw and heard, smelled and touched him, they remained distant. Only later when he was gone could his true Spirit reveal itself to them. In his absence a new and more intimate presence became possible, a presence which nurtured and sustained in the midst of tribulations and which created the desire to see him again. The great mystery of the divine revelation is that God entered into intimacy with us not only by Christ's coming, but also by his leaving. Indeed, it is in Christ's absence that our intimacy with him is so profound that we can say he dwells in us, call him our food and drink, and experience him as the center of our being.

That this is far from a theoretical idea becomes clear in the lives of people like Dietrich Bonhoeffer and Alfred Delp who, while in Nazi prisons waiting for death, experienced Christ's presence in the midst of his absence. Bonhoeffer writes: "The God who is with us is the God who forsakes us (Mark 15:34)....Before God and with God we live without God." Thus the memory of Jesus Christ is much more than the bringing to mind of past redemptive events. It is a life-giving memory, a memory which sustains and nurtures us here and now and so gives us a real sense of being rooted amid the many crises of daily life.

✠

In Jesus no division existed between his words and his actions, between what he said and what he did. Jesus' words were his action, his words were events. They not only spoke about changes, cures, new life, but they actually created them. In this sense, Jesus is truly the Word made flesh; in that Word all is created and by that Word all is recreated.

Saintliness means living without division between word and action. If I would truly live in my own life the word I am speaking, my spoken words would become actions, and miracles would happen whenever I opened my mouth.

Prayer

We give thanks to you, God,
we give thanks to you,
as we call upon your name,
as we recount your wonders.

But I shall speak out for ever,
shall make music for the God of Jacob.

—Ps. 75:1, 9

⇥ Thursday of the Third Week in Lent ⇤

Anyone who is not with me is against me; and anyone who does not gather in with me throws away.

—Luke 11:23

✠

The spiritual life is a gift. It is the gift of the Holy Spirit, who lifts us up into the kingdom of God's love. But to say that being lifted up into the kingdom of love is a divine gift does not mean that we wait passively until the gift is offered to us. Jesus tells us to set our hearts on the kingdom. Setting our hearts on something involves not only serious aspiration but also strong determination. A spiritual life requires human effort. The forces that keep pulling us back into a worry-filled life are far from easy to overcome.

"How hard it is," Jesus exclaims, " . . . to enter the kingdom of God!" (Mark 10:23). And to convince us of the need for hard work, he says, "If anyone wants to be a follower of mine, let him renounce himself and take up his cross and follow me" (Matt. 16:24).

Here we touch the question of discipline in the spiritual life. A spiritual life without discipline is impossible. Discipline is the other side of discipleship. The practice of a spiritual discipline makes us more sensitive to the small, gentle voice of God. The prophet Elijah did not encounter God in the mighty wind or in the earthquake or in the fire, but in the small voice (see 1 Kings 19:9–13). Through the practice of a spiritual discipline we become attentive to that small voice and willing to respond when we hear it.

✠

73

From all that I said about our worried, over-filled lives, it is clear that we are usually surrounded by so much inner and outer noise that it is hard to truly hear our God when he is speaking to us. We have often become deaf, unable to know when God calls us and unable to understand in which direction he calls us. Thus our lives have become absurd. In the word *absurd* we find the Latin word *surdus*, which means "deaf." A spiritual life requires discipline because we need to learn to listen to God, who constantly speaks but whom we seldom hear. When, however, we learn to listen, our lives become obedient lives. The word *obedient* comes from the Latin word *audire*, which means " listening. " A spiritual discipline is necessary in order to move slowly from an absurd to an obedient life, from a life filled with noisy worries to a life in which there is some free inner space where we can listen to our God and follow his guidance. Jesus' life was a life of obedience. He was always listening to the Father, always attentive to his voice, always alert for his directions. Jesus was "all ear." That is true prayer: being all ear for God. The core of all prayer is indeed listening, obediently standing in the presence of God.

A spiritual discipline, therefore, is the concentrated effort to create some inner and outer space in our lives, where this obedience can be practiced. Through a spiritual discipline we prevent the world from filling our lives to such an extent that there is no place left to listen. A spiritual discipline sets us free to pray or, to say it better, allows the Spirit of God to pray in us.

Prayer

Almighty God,
grant that we may heed the call of your grace
and ready ourselves all the more fervently
to celebrate the mysteries of Easter,
as the feast of our redemption comes closer and closer.

❧ Friday of the Third Week in Lent ❧

You must love the Lord your God with all your heart, with all your soul, with all your mind and with all your strength.

— Mark 12:30

✠

To live a spiritual life is to live in the presence of God. This very straightforward truth was brought home to me forcefully by Brother Lawrence, a French Carmelite brother who lived in the seventeenth century. The book *The Practice of the Presence of God* contains four conversations with Brother Lawrence and fifteen letters by him.

He writes: "It is not necessary for being with God to be always at church. We may make an oratory of our heart wherein to retire from time to time to converse with him in meekness, humility, and love. Everyone is capable of such familiar conversation with God, some more, some less. He knows what we can do. Let us begin, then. Perhaps he expects but one generous resolution on our part. Have courage."

"I know that for the right practice of it [the presence of God] the heart must be empty of all other things, because God will possess the heart *alone;* and as he cannot possess it alone without emptying it of all besides, so neither can he act *there*, and do in it what pleases, unless it be left vacant to him."

Brother Lawrence's message, in all its simplicity, is very profound. For him who has become close to God, all is one. Only God counts, and in God all people and all things are embraced with love. To live in the presence of God, however, is to live with purity of heart, with simple-mindedness, and with total acceptance of his will. That,

indeed, demands a choice, a decision, and great courage.
It is a sign of true holiness.

Prayer

Dear Lord, you once said,
"The will of him who sent me
is that I should lose nothing
of all that he has given to me."
These words are a source of consolation this day.
They show that you are doing all that can be done
to keep me in your love.
They demonstrate that indeed
you entered this world to save me,
to free me from the bonds of evil and sin,
and to lead me to your Father's house.
They reveal that you are willing
to struggle against the strong powers
which pull me away from you.
Lord, you want to keep me, hold onto me,
fight for me, protect me, help me, support me,
comfort me, and present me to your Father.
It indeed is your divine task not to lose me!
And yet I am free.
I can separate myself from you,
and you will never take this freedom away from me.
Oh, what a wonder of love,
what a mystery of divine grace!
Please, Lord, let me freely choose for your love
so that I will not be lost to you.
Amen.

✠ Saturday of the Third Week in Lent ✠

Come, let us return to Yahweh.
He has rent us and he will heal us;
he has struck us and he will bind up our wounds;
— Hos. 6:1, 2

✠

Living a spiritual life requires a change of heart, a conversion. Such a conversion may be marked by a sudden inner change, or it can take place through a long, quiet process of transformation. But it always involves an inner experience of oneness. We realize that we are in the center, and that from there all that is and all that takes place can be seen and understood as part of the mystery of God's life with us. Our conflicts and pains, our tasks and promises, our families and friends, our activities and projects, our hopes and aspirations, no longer appear to us as a fatiguing variety of things which we can barely keep together, but rather as affirmations and revelations of the new life of the Spirit in us. "All these other things," which so occupied and preoccupied us, now come as gifts or challenges that strengthen and deepen the new life which we have discovered. This does not mean that the spiritual life makes things easier or takes our struggles and pains away. The lives of Jesus' disciples clearly show that suffering does not diminish because of conversion. Sometimes it even becomes more intense. But our attention is no longer directed to the "more or less." What matters is to listen attentively to the Spirit and to go obediently where we are being led, whether to a joyful or a painful place.

Poverty, pain, struggle, anguish, agony, and even inner darkness may continue to be part of our experience. They may even be God's way of purifying us. But life is no longer boring, resentful, depressing, or lonely because we have come to know that everything that happens is part of our way to the house of the Father.

Prayer

O Lord, this holy season of Lent is passing quickly.
I entered into it with fear,
but also with great expectations.
I hoped for a great breakthrough,
a powerful conversion, a real change of heart;
I wanted Easter to be a day so full of light
that not even a trace of darkness
would be left in my soul.
But I know that you do not come to your people
with thunder and lightning.
Even St. Paul and St. Francis
journeyed through much darkness
before they could see your light.
Let me be thankful for your gentle way.
I know you are at work.
I know you will not leave me alone.
I know you are quickening me for Easter —
but in a way fitting to my own history
and my own temperament.

I pray that these last three weeks,
in which you invite me to enter more fully
into the mystery of your passion,
will bring me a greater desire to follow you
on the way that you create for me
and to accept the cross that you give to me.
Let me die to the desire
to choose my own way and select my own cross.

You do not want to make me a hero
but a servant who loves you.

Be with me tomorrow and in the days to come,
and let me experience your gentle presence.
Amen.

"Lord, you know everything; you know I love you." Jesus said to him, "Feed my sheep."

—John 21:17

⊰⊱ Fourth Sunday in Lent ⊰⊱

God does not see as human beings see; they look at appearances but Yahweh looks at the heart.

— 1 Sam. 16:7

✠

Secularity is a way of being dependent on the responses of our milieu. The secular or false self is the self which is fabricated, as Thomas Merton says, by social compulsions. "Compulsive" is indeed the best adjective for the false self. It points to the need for ongoing and increasing affirmation. Who am I? I am the one who is liked, praised, admired, disliked, hated, or despised.... The compulsion manifests itself in the lurking fear of failing and the steady urge to prevent this by gathering more of the same — more work, more money, more friends.

These very compulsions are at the basis of the two main enemies of the spiritual life: anger and greed. They are the inner side of a secular life, the sour fruits of our worldly dependencies.

✠

It is not so strange that Anthony and his fellow monks considered it a spiritual disaster to accept passively the tenets and values of their society. They had come to appreciate how hard it is not only for the individual Christian but also for the church itself to escape the seductive compulsions of the world. What was their response? They escaped from the sinking ship and swam for their lives. And the place of salvation is called desert, the place of solitude....

Solitude is the furnace of transformation. Without solitude we remain victims of our society and continue to

be entangled in the illusions of the false self. Jesus himself entered into this furnace. There he was tempted with
the three compulsions of the world: to be relevant ("turn
stones into loaves"), to be spectacular ("throw yourself
down"), and to be powerful ("I will give you all these
kingdoms"). There he affirmed God as the only source
of his identity ("You must worship the Lord your God
and serve him alone"). Solitude is the place of the great
struggle and the great encounter — the struggle against
the compulsions of the false self, and the encounter with
the loving God who offers himself as the substance of the
new self.

✠

Our heart is at the center of our being human. There our
deepest thoughts, intuitions, emotions, and decisions find
their source. But it's also there that we are often most
alienated from ourselves. We know little or nothing of
our own heart. We keep our distance, as though we were
afraid of it. What is most intimate is also what frightens us most. Where we are most ourselves, we are often
strangers to ourselves. That is the painful part of our being human. We fail to know our hidden centers; and so
we live and die often without knowing who we really are.
If we ask ourselves why we think, feel, and act in such
or such a way, we often have no answer, thus proving to
be strangers in our own house. The mystery of the spiritual life is that Jesus desires to meet us in the seclusion
of our own heart, to make his love known to us there, to
free us from our fears and to make our own deepest self
known to us. In the privacy of our heart, therefore, we can
learn not only to know Jesus but, through Jesus, ourselves
as well.

Prayer

Almighty God,
your eternal word is the true light
that enlightens every human being.
Heal the blindness of our hearts,
that we may discern what is right
and love you sincerely.

He went again to Cana in Galilee, where he had changed the water into wine. And there was a court official whose son was ill at Capernaum; hearing that Jesus had arrived in Galilee from Judaea, he went and asked him to come and cure his son, as he was at the point of death. Jesus said to him, "Unless you see signs and portents you will not believe!" "Sir," answered the official, "Come down before my child dies." "Go home," said Jesus, "your son will live." The man believed what Jesus had said and went on his way home.

—John 4:46–50

The descending way of Jesus, painful as it is, is God's most radical attempt to convince us that everything we long for is indeed given us. What he asks of us is to have faith in that love. The word "faith" is often understood as accepting something you can't understand. People often say: "Such and such can't be explained, you simply have to believe it." However, when Jesus talks about faith, he means first of all to trust unreservedly that you are loved, so that you can abandon every false way of obtaining love. That's why Jesus tells Nicodemus that, through faith in the descending love of God, we will be set free from anxiety and violence and will find eternal life.

The mystery of God's love is not that he takes our pains away, but that he first wants to share them with us. Out of this divine solidarity comes new life. Jesus' being moved in the center of his being by human pain is indeed a movement toward new life. God is our God, the God of the living. In his divine womb life is always born again.... The truly good news is that God is not a distant God, a God to be feared and avoided, a God of revenge, but a God who is moved by our pains and participates in the fullness of the human struggle.

Prayer

INTEGRITY and generosity are marks of Yahweh
for he brings sinners back to the path.

JUDICIOUSLY he guides the humble,
instructing the poor in his way.

ADORATION I offer, Yahweh,
to you, my God.

—Ps. 25:8, 9, 10

❧ Tuesday of the Fourth Week in Lent ❧

Jesus met him in the Temple and said, "Now you are well again, do not sin any more."

—John 5:14

✠

Prayer heals. Not just the answer to prayer. When we give up our competition with God and offer God every part of our heart, holding back nothing at all, we come to know God's love for us and discover how safe we are in his embrace. Once we know again that God has not rejected us, but keeps us close to his heart, we can find again the joy of living, even though God might guide our life in a different direction from our desires.

✠

I hardly remember what it was, but a small critical remark and a few irritations during my work in the bakery were enough to tumble me head-over-heels into a deep, morose mood. Many hostile feelings were triggered and in a long sequence of morbid associations, I felt worse and worse about myself, my past, my work, and all the people who came to mind. But happily I saw myself tumbling and was amazed how little was needed to lose my peace of mind and to pull my whole world out of perspective. Oh, how vulnerable I am.

The milieu of this place full of prayerful people prevents me from acting out, from getting angry, from bursting open. I can sit down and see how quickly the little empty place of peace in my heart is filled again with rocks and garbage falling down from all sides.

It is hard to pray in such a mood. But still during Terce, the short prayer immediately after work, standing outside in our dirty work clothes, we read: "Is anyone among you in trouble? He should turn to prayer." Indeed prayer is the only real way to clean my heart and to create new space. I am discovering how important that inner space is. When it is there it seems that I can receive many concerns of others in it without becoming depressed. When I sense that inner quiet place, I can pray for many others and feel a very intimate relationship with them. There even seems to be room for the thousands of suffering people in prisons and in the deserts of North Africa. Sometimes I feel as if my heart expands from my parents traveling in Indonesia to my friends in Los Angeles and from the Chilean prisons to the parishes in Brooklyn.

Now I know that it is not I who pray but the spirit of God who prays in me. Indeed, when God's glory dwells in me, there is nothing too far away, nothing too painful, nothing too strange or too familiar that it cannot contain and renew by its touch. Every time I recognize the glory of God in me and give it space to manifest itself to me, all that is human can be brought there and nothing will be the same again. Once in a while I just know it: Of course, God hears my prayer. He himself prays in me and touches the whole world with his love right here and now.

Prayer

O Lord Jesus Christ,
you who forgave the sins of the paralytic
before you let him walk again,
I pray that [this Lenten period] may make me more
    aware of your forgiving presence in my life
and less concerned about performing well in the eyes
    of my world.
Let me recognize you
at that virginal point in the depth of my heart

where you dwell and heal me.
Let me experience you in that center of my being
from which you want to teach and guide me.
Let me know you as my loving brother
who holds nothing —
not even my worst sins —
against me,
but who wants to touch me in a gentle embrace.
Take away the many fears, suspicions, and doubts
by which I prevent you from being my Lord,
and give me the courage and freedom to appear naked
    and vulnerable
in the light of your presence,
confident in your unfathomable mercy.

I know how great my resistance is,
how quickly I choose the darkness instead of the light.
But I also know that you keep calling me into the light,
where I can see not only my sins
but your gracious face as well.
Be with me every hour of my days.

Praise and glory to you, now and forever.
Amen.

⋇ Wednesday of the Fourth Week in Lent ⋇

In all truth I tell you,
by himself the Son can do nothing;
he can do only what he sees the Father doing:
and whatever the Father does the Son does too.
—John 5:19

✠

[Jesus'] obedience means a total, fearless listening to his loving Father. Between the Father and the Son there is only love. Everything that belongs to the Father, he entrusts to the Son (Luke 10:22), and everything the Son has received, he returns to the Father. The Father opens himself totally to the Son and puts everything in his hands: all knowledge (John 12:50), all glory (John 8:54), all power (John 5:19–21). And the Son opens himself totally to the Father and thus returns everything into his Father's hands. "I came from the Father and have come into the world and now I leave the world to go to the Father" (John 16:28).

This inexhaustible love between the Father and the Son includes and yet transcends all forms of love known to us. It includes the love of a father and mother, a brother and sister, a husband and wife, a teacher and friend. But it also goes far beyond the many limited and limiting human experiences of love we know. It is a caring yet demanding love. It is a supportive yet severe love. It is a gentle yet strong love. It is a love that gives life yet accepts death. In this divine love Jesus was sent into the world, to this divine love Jesus offered himself on the cross. This all-embracing love, which epitomizes the relationship between the Father and the Son, is a divine Person, coequal with the Father and the Son. It has a personal name. It is called the

Holy Spirit. The Father loves the Son and pours himself out in the Son. The Son is loved by the Father and returns all he is to the Father. The Spirit is love itself, eternally embracing the Father and the Son.

This eternal community of love is the center and source of Jesus' spiritual life, a life of uninterrupted attentiveness to the Father in the Spirit of love. It is from this life that Jesus' ministry grows. His eating and fasting, his praying and acting, his traveling and resting, his preaching and teaching, his exorcising and healing, were all done in this Spirit of love. We will never understand the full meaning of Jesus' richly varied ministry unless we see how the many things are rooted in the one thing: listening to the Father in the intimacy of perfect love. When we see this, we will also realize that the goal of Jesus' ministry is nothing less than to bring us into this most intimate community.

✠

Today in the Gospel reading of the liturgy, Jesus reveals that everything he does is done in relationship with his Father....

Jesus' words have a special meaning for me. I must live in an ongoing relationship with Jesus and through him with the Father. This relationship is the core of the spiritual life. This relationship prevents my life from being consumed by "keeping up" with things. This relationship prevents my days from becoming boring, fatiguing, draining, depressing, and frustrating. If all that I do can become more and more an expression of my participation in God's life of total giving and receiving in love, everything else will be blessed and will lose its fragmented quality. This does not mean that everything will become easy and harmonious. There will still be much agony, but when connected with God's own agony, even my agony can lead to life.

Prayer

And so, I pray to you, Yahweh,
  at the time of your favor;
in your faithful love answer me,
  in the constancy of your saving power.

Answer me, Yahweh, for your faithful love is generous;
in your tenderness turn towards me;
do not turn away from your servant.

—Ps. 69:13, 16

⊰ Thursday of the Fourth Week in Lent ⊱

How can you believe,
since you look to each other for glory
and are not concerned
with the glory that comes from the one God?
—John 5:44

✠

I have gradually become aware how central this word
[*glory*] is in John's Gospel. There is God's glory, the right
glory that leads to life. And there is human glory, the
vain glory that leads to death. All through his Gospel John
shows how we are tempted to prefer vain glory over the
glory that comes from God.

Human glory is always connected with some form of
competition. Human glory is the result of being considered better, faster, more beautiful, more powerful, or more
successful than others. Glory conferred by people is glory
which results from being favorably compared to other people. The better our scores on the scoreboard of life, the
more glory we receive. This glory comes with upward mobility. The higher we climb on the ladder of success, the
more glory we collect. But this same glory also creates our
darkness. Human glory, based on competition, leads to
rivalry; rivalry carries within it the beginning of violence;
and violence is the way to death. Thus human glory proves
to be vain glory, false glory, mortal glory.

✠

How then do we come to see and receive God's glory? In
his Gospel, John shows that God chose to reveal his glory
to us in his humiliation. That is the good, but also disturb-
ing, news. God, in his infinite wisdom, chose to reveal his

divinity to us not through competition, but through compassion, that is, through suffering with us. God chose the way of downward mobility. Every time Jesus speaks about being glorified and giving glory, he always refers to his humiliation and death. It is through the way of the cross that Jesus gives glory to God, receives glory from God, and makes God's glory known to us. The glory of the resurrection can never be separated from the glory of the cross. The risen Lord always shows us his wounds.

Thus the glory of God stands in contrast to the glory of people. People seek glory by moving upward. God reveals his glory by moving downward. If we truly want to see the glory of God, we must move downward with Jesus. This is the deepest reason for living in solidarity with poor, oppressed, and handicapped people. They are the ones through whom God's glory can manifest itself to us. They show us the way to God, the way to salvation.

Prayer

How often have I lived through these weeks
without paying much attention
to penance, fasting, and prayer?
How often have I missed
the spiritual fruits of this season
without even being aware of it?
But how can I ever really celebrate Easter
without observing Lent?
How can I rejoice fully in your resurrection
when I have avoided participating in your death?

Yes, Lord, I have to die —
with you, through you, and in you —
and thus become ready to recognize you
when you appear to me in your resurrection.
There is so much in me that needs to die:

false attachments, greed and anger,
impatience and stinginess.
O Lord, I am self-centered,
concerned about myself, my career, my future,
my name and future, my name and fame.

I see clearly now how little I have died with you,
really gone your way and been faithful to it.
O Lord, make this Lenten season
different from the other ones.
Let me find you again.
Amen.

⋈ Friday of the Fourth Week in Lent ⋈

You know me and you know where I came from.
Yet I have not come of my own accord:
but he who sent me is true;
You do not know him,
but I know him
because I have my being from him
and it was he who sent me.

—John 7:28, 29

✠

Fellowship with Jesus Christ is not a commitment to suffer as much as possible, but a commitment to listen with him to God's love without fear. . . .

We are often tempted to "explain" suffering in terms of "the will of God." Not only can this evoke anger and frustration, but also it is false. "God's will" is not a label that can be put on unhappy situations. God wants to bring joy not pain, peace not war, healing not suffering. Therefore, instead of declaring anything and everything to be the will of God, we must be willing to ask ourselves where in the midst of our pains and sufferings we can discern the loving presence of God.

When, however, we discover that our obedient listening leads us to our suffering neighbors, we can go to them in the joyful knowledge that love brings us there. We are poor listeners because we are afraid that there is something other than love in God. This is not so strange since we seldom, if ever, experience love without a taint of jealousy, resentment, revenge, or even hatred. Often we see love surrounded by limitations and conditions. We tend to doubt what presents itself to us as love and are always on guard, prepared for disappointments. . . .

For this reason we find it hard simply to listen or to obey. But Jesus truly listened and obeyed because only he knew the love of his Father: "Not that anybody has seen the Father, except the one who comes from God: he has seen the Father" (John 6:46). "You do not know him, but I know him because I have come from him . . . " (John 7:28–29).

He came to include us in his divine obedience. He wanted to lead us to the Father so that we could enjoy the same intimacy he did. When we come to recognize that in and through Jesus we are called to be daughters and sons of God and to listen to him, our loving Father, with total trust and surrender, we will also see that we are invited to be no less compassionate than Jesus himself. When obedience becomes our first and only concern, then we too can move into the world with compassion and feel the suffering of the world so deeply that through our compassion we can give new life to others.

✠

The world in which we live today and about whose suffering we know so much seems more than ever a world from which Christ has withdrawn himself. How can I believe that in this world we are constantly being prepared to receive the Spirit? Still, I think that this is exactly the message of hope. God has not withdrawn himself. He sent his Son to share our human condition and the Son sent us his Spirit to lead us into the intimacy of his divine life. It is in the midst of the chaotic suffering of humanity that the Holy Spirit, the Spirit of Love, makes himself visible. But can we recognize his presence?

Prayer

Merciful God,
you know our weakness and distress.
Yet the weaker we are,
the stronger is your help.
Grant that we may accept with joy and gratitude
the gift of this time of grace,
and bear witness to your work in our lives.

⊰⊱ Saturday of the Fourth Week in Lent ⊰⊱

Some of the crowd who had been listening said, "He is indeed the prophet," and some said, "He is the Christ," but others said, "Would the Christ come from Galilee?"

—John 7:40, 41

✠

The Gospel today reveals that Jesus not only had good, faithful friends willing to follow him wherever he went and fierce enemies who couldn't wait to get rid of him, but also many sympathizers who were attracted, but afraid at the same time.

The rich young man loved Jesus but couldn't give up his wealth to follow him. Nicodemus admired Jesus but was afraid to lose the respect of his own colleagues. I am becoming more and more aware of the importance of looking at these fearful sympathizers because that is the group I find myself mostly gravitating toward....

To his colleagues, the Pharisees, Nicodemus said, "Our Law does not allow us to pass judgment on anyone without first giving him a hearing and discovering what he is doing" (John 7:51). These are careful words. They are spoken to people who hate Jesus. But they are spoken on their terms. They say, "Even if you hate Jesus and desire to kill him, do not lose your dignity, follow your own rules." Nicodemus said it to save Jesus, but he didn't want to lose his friends. It didn't work. He was ridiculed by his friends: "Are you a Galilean too? Go into the matter, and see for yourself: prophets do not arise from Galilee!" His personal and professional identity are attacked.

It is such a familiar scene. I have spoken like Nicodemus in episcopal committees and faculty meetings many times. Instead of speaking directly about my love for Jesus, I make a smart remark suggesting that maybe my friends should look at another side of the question. They usually respond by saying I have not studied my sources well enough, or that I seem to have some sentimental attachment that got in the way of a truly professional approach. Those who have said these things have had the power of right thinking and thus forced me to silence. But it has been fear that has prevented me from speaking from the heart and risking rejection.

Nicodemus deserves all my attention.

Prayer

Dear Lord,
show me your kindness and your gentleness,
you who are meek and humble of heart.
So often I say to myself, "The Lord loves me."

Yet time and again I have to confess
that I have not let your love descend fully
from my mind into my heart.

In the coming weeks, O Lord,
I will be able to see again
how much you indeed love me.
Let these weeks become an opportunity for me
to let go of all my resistances to your love
and an occasion for you to call me closer to you.
Amen.

⊰ Passion Sunday ⊱

I am the resurrection.
Anyone who believes in me, even though that person
  dies, will live,
and whoever lives and believes in me
will never die.

—John 11:25, 26

✙

Finding new life through suffering and death: that is the core of the good news. Jesus has lived out that liberating way before us and has made it the great sign. Human beings are forever wanting to see signs: marvellous, extraordinary, sensational events that can distract them a little from hard reality.... We would like to see something marvellous, something exceptional, something that interrupts the ordinary life of every day. That way, if only for a moment, we can play at hide-and-seek. But to those who say to Jesus: "Master, ... we should like to see a sign from you," he replies: "It is an evil and unfaithful generation that asks for a sign! The only sign it will be given is the sign of the prophet Jonah. For as Jonah remained in the belly of the sea monster for three days and three nights, so will the Son of Man be in the heart of the earth for three days and three nights."

From this one can see what the authentic sign is: not some sensational miracle but the suffering, death, burial, and resurrection of Jesus. The great sign, which can be understood only by those who are willing to follow Jesus, is the sign of Jonah, who also wanted to run away from reality but was summoned back by God to fulfil his arduous task to the end. To look suffering and death straight in the face *and* to go through them oneself in the hope of a new God-given life: that is the sign of Jesus and of every human being who wishes to lead a spiritual life in imitation of him. It is the sign of the cross: the sign of suffering and death, but also of the hope for total renewal.

✠

Even though Jesus went directly against the human inclination to avoid suffering and death, his followers realized that it was better to live the truth with open eyes than to live their lives in illusion.

Suffering and death belong to the narrow road of Jesus. Jesus does not glorify them, or call them beautiful, good, or something to be desired. Jesus does not call for heroism or suicidal self-sacrifice. No, Jesus invites us to look at the reality of our existence and reveals this harsh reality as the way to new life. The core message of Jesus is that real joy and peace can never be reached while bypassing suffering and death, but only by going right through them.

We could say: We really have no choice. Indeed, who escapes suffering and death? Yet there is still a choice. We can deny the reality of life, or we can face it. When we face it not in despair, but with the eyes of Jesus, we discover that where we least expect it, something is hidden that holds a promise stronger than death itself. Jesus lived his life with the trust that God's love is stronger than death and that death therefore does not have the last word. He invites us to face the painful reality of our existence with the same trust. This is what Lent is all about.

Prayer

You have the words of eternal life,
you are food and drink,
you are the Way, the Truth, and the Life.
You are the light that shines in the darkness,
the lamp on the lampstand, the house on the hilltop.
You are the perfect Icon of God.
In and through you I can see the Heavenly Father,
and with you I can find my way to him.

Be my Lord, my Savior, my Redeemer,
my Guide, my Consoler, my Comforter,
my Hope, my Joy, and my Peace.
To you I want to give all that I am.
Let me give you all —
all I have, think, do, and feel.
It is yours, O Lord.
Please accept it and make it fully your own.
Amen.

❧ Monday in Passion Week ❦

The scribes and Pharisees brought a woman along who had been caught committing adultery; and making her stand there in the middle they said to Jesus, "Master, this woman was caught in the very act of committing adultery, and in the Law Moses has ordered us to stone women of this kind. What have you got to say?" They asked him this as a test, looking for an accusation to use against him. But Jesus bent down and started writing on the ground with his finger. As they persisted with their question, he straightened up and said, "Let the one among you who is guiltless be the first to throw a stone at her."

—John 8:3–7

✠

The truly good news is that God is not a distant God, a God to be feared and avoided, a God of revenge, but a God who is moved by our pains and participates in the fullness of the human struggle....

God is a compassionate God. This means, first of all, that he is a God who has chosen to be God-with-us....

As soon as we call God, "God-with-us," we enter into a new relationship of intimacy with him. By calling him Immanuel, we recognize that he has committed himself to live in solidarity with us, to share our joys and pains, to defend and protect us, and to suffer all of life with us. The God-with-us is a close God, a God whom we call our refuge, our stronghold, our wisdom, and even, more intimately, our helper, our shepherd, our love. We will never really know God as a compassionate God if we do not understand with our heart and mind that "he lived among us" (John 1:14).

✠

How do we know that God is our God and not a stranger, an outsider, a passerby?

We know this because in Jesus God's compassion became visible to us. Jesus not only said, "Be compassionate as your Father is compassionate," but he also was the concrete embodiment of this divine compassion in our world. Jesus' response to the ignorant, the hungry, the blind, the lepers, the widows, and all those who came to him with their suffering, flowed from the divine compassion which led God to become one of us. We need to pay close attention to Jesus' words and actions if we are to gain insight into the mystery of this divine compassion. We would misunderstand the many miraculous stories in the Gospels if we were to be impressed simply by the fact that sick and tormented people were suddenly liberated from their pains. If this were indeed the central event of these stories, a cynic might rightly remark that most people during Jesus' day were *not* cured and that those who were cured only made it worse for those who were not. What is important here is not the cure of the sick, but the deep compassion that moved Jesus to these cures.

Prayer

Lord, you have not come to judge the world,
but to save the world:
anyone who rejects you and refuses your words
has his judge already:
the word itself that you have spoken
will be his judge on the last day.

— After John 12:47–48

When you have lifted up the Son of man,
then you will know that I am He
and that I do nothing of my own accord.
What I say
is what the Father has taught me;
he who sent me is with me,
and has not left me to myself,
for I always do what pleases him.

—John 8:28, 29

✠

The whole of Jesus' ministry pointed away from himself to the Father who had sent him. To his disciples Jesus said, "The words I say to you I do not speak as from myself; it is the Father, living in me, who is doing this work" (John 14:10). Jesus, the Word of God made flesh, spoke not to attract attention to himself but to show the way to his Father: "I came from the Father and have come into the world and now I leave the world to go to the Father (John 16:28). I am going to prepare a place for you . . . so that where I am you may be too" (John 14:2–3). In order to be a ministry in the Name of Jesus, our ministry must also point beyond our words to the unspeakable mystery of God. . . .

If it is true that the word of Scripture should lead us into the silence of God, then we must be careful to use that word not simply as an interesting or motivating word, but as a word that creates the boundaries within which we can listen to the loving, caring, gentle presence of God.

✠

Jesus said: "Let us go . . . to the neighboring country towns, so that I can preach there too, because that is why I came."

The words which Jesus spoke in these neighboring boring country towns were born in the intimacy with the
Father. They were words of comfort and of condemna-
tion, words of hope and of warning, words of unity and of
division. He dared to speak these challenging words because he did not seek his own glory: "If I were to seek my
own glory," he says, "that would be no glory at all; my
glory is conferred by the Father, by the one of whom you
say 'He is our God,' although you do not know him" (John
8:54). Within a few years Jesus' words brought about his
rejection and death.

✠

Jesus learned obedience from what he suffered. This means
that the pains and struggles of which Jesus became part
made him listen more perfectly to God. In and through
his sufferings, he came to know God and could respond
to his call. Maybe there are no better words than these to
summarize the meaning of the option for the poor. Entering into the suffering of the poor is the way to become
obedient, that is, a listener to God. Suffering accepted and
shared in love breaks down our selfish defenses and sets
us free to accept God's guidance.

✠

Nothing is real without deriving its reality from God. This
was the great discovery of St. Francis when he suddenly
saw the whole world in God's hands and wondered why
God didn't drop it. St. Augustine, St. Teresa of Avila,
St. John Vianney, and all the saints are saints precisely because for them the order of being was turned around and
they saw, felt, and — above all — knew with their heart
that outside God nothing is, nothing breathes, nothing
moves, and nothing lives.

Prayer

Lord Jesus Christ,
this is the will of your Father
that whoever sees you and believes in you
should have eternal life,
and that you should raise that person up on the last day.

— After John 6:40

⊰❦ Wednesday in Passion Week ❦⊱

*If you make my word your home
you will indeed be my disciples;
you will come to know the truth,
and the truth will set you free.*
—John 8:31

He became like us so that we might become like him. He did not cling to his equality with God, but emptied himself and became as we are so that we might become like him and thus share in his divine life.

This radical transformation of our lives is the work of the Holy Spirit. The disciples could hardly comprehend what Jesus meant. As long as Jesus was present to them in the flesh, they did not yet recognize his full presence in the Spirit. That is why Jesus said: "It is for your own good that I am going because unless I go, the Advocate [the Holy Spirit] will not come to you; but if I do go, I will send him to you" (John 16:7)....

Jesus sends the Spirit so that we may be led to the full truth of the divine life. *Truth* does not mean an idea, concept, or doctrine, but the true relationship. To be led into the truth is to be led into the same relationship that Jesus has with the Father; it is to enter into a divine betrothal.

Thus Pentecost is the completion of Jesus' mission. On Pentecost the fullness of Jesus' ministry becomes visible. When the Holy Spirit descends upon the disciples and dwells with them, their lives are transformed into Christ-like lives, lives shaped by the same love that exists between the Father and Son. The spiritual life is indeed a life in which we are lifted up to become partakers of the divine life.

To be lifted up into the divine life of the Father, the Son, and the Holy Spirit does not mean, however, to be taken out of the world. On the contrary, those who have entered into the spiritual life are precisely the ones who are sent into the world to continue and fulfill the work that Jesus began. The spiritual life does not remove us from the world but leads us deeper into it. Jesus says to his Father, "As you sent me into the world, I have sent them into the world" (John 17:18). He makes it clear that precisely because his disciples no longer belong to the world, they can live in the world as he did....

Life in the Spirit of Jesus is therefore a life in which Jesus' coming into the world — his incarnation, his death, and resurrection — is lived out by those who have entered into the same obedient relationship to the Father which marked Jesus' own life. Having become sons and daughters as Jesus was Son, our lives become a continuation of Jesus' mission.

✠

The interior life, Gustavo Gutiérrez said, does not refer to the psychological reality that one reaches through introspection, but is the life lived free from the constraining power of the law in the Pauline sense. It is a life free to love. Thus the spiritual life is the place of true freedom. When we are able to throw off the compulsions and coercions that come from outside of us and can allow the Holy Spirit, God's love, to be our only guide, then we can live a truly free, interior, and spiritual life.

Prayer

Dear Lord, you are the Truth.
When I keep myself rooted in you,
I will live in the Truth.
Help me, Lord, to live a truthful life,
a life in which I am guided
not by popularity, public opinion,
current fashion, or convenient formulations
but by a knowledge that comes from knowing you.

There may be times during which holding onto the
    Truth is hard and painful,
and leads to oppression, persecution, and death.
Be with me, Lord, if that time ever comes.
Let me then experience
that to hold onto the Truth means to hold onto you,
that Love and Truth can never be separated,
and that to live truthfully is the same as being faithful
to a loving relationship.

Lord, bring me always closer to you.
Amen.

⋙ Thursday in Passion Week ⋘

In all truth I tell you,
whoever keeps my word
will never see death.
—John 8:51

✠

But we, too, are subject to the temptations of this world,
the temptations of greed and lust, violence and revenge,
hatred and destruction. We are not immune to the powers
of the beasts. Therefore we have to help each other to keep
our hearts and minds directed toward the Son of Man, so
that we will recognize him when he comes and will be
free to stand with confidence before him (see Luke 21:36).
We have to keep ourselves and each other anchored in his
words, because "heaven and earth will pass away, but my
words will never pass away" (Luke 21:33). It is on that
eternal Word, who became flesh and lived among us, that
our hope is built.

✠

You and I, both, are called to be disciples of Jesus. . . . What
counts is being attentive at all times to the voice of God's
love inviting us to obey, that is, to listen with an attentive
heart.

How can we keep listening to this voice in a world
which does its best to distract us and get our attention for
seemingly more urgent matters? . . .

First of all, listen to the Church. I know that that isn't
a popular bit of advice at a time and in a country where
the Church is frequently seen more as an "obstacle" in the
way rather than as the "way" to Jesus. Nevertheless, I'm
profoundly convinced that the greatest spiritual danger for

our times is the separation of Jesus from the Church. The Church is the body of the Lord. Without Jesus there can be no Church; and without the Church we cannot stay united with Jesus. I've yet to meet anyone who has come closer to Jesus by forsaking the Church. To listen to the Church is to listen to the Lord of the Church. Specifically, this means taking part in the Church's liturgical life. Advent, Christmas, Lent, Easter, Ascension, and Pentecost; these seasons and feasts teach you to know Jesus better and better, and unite you more and more intimately with the divine life he offers you in the Church.

The Eucharist is the heart of the Church's life. It's there that you hear the life-giving Gospel and receive the gifts that sustain that life within you. The best assurance that you'll keep listening to the Church is your regular participation in the Eucharist.

Prayer

O God, it is impossible to believe you
without faith,
since anyone who comes to you
must believe that you exist
and reward those who seek you.

— After Heb. 11:6

⚜ Friday in Passion Week ⚜

"I have shown you many good works from my Father; for which of these are you stoning me?"

—John 10:32

✠

When Jesus saw the crowd harassed and dejected like sheep without a shepherd, he felt with them in the center of his being (Matt. 9:36). When he saw the blind, the paralyzed, and the deaf being brought to him from all directions, he trembled from within and experienced their pains in his own heart (Matt. 14:14). When he noticed that the thousands who had followed him for days were tired and hungry, he said, I am moved with compassion (Mark 8:2). And so it was with the two blind men who called after him (Matt. 9:27), the leper who fell to his knees in front of him (Mark 1:41), and the widow of Nain who was burying her only son (Luke 7:13). They moved him, they made him feel with all his intimate sensibilities the depth of their sorrow. He became lost with the lost, hungry with the hungry, and sick with the sick. In him, all suffering was sensed with a perfect sensitivity. The great mystery revealed to us in this is that Jesus, who is the sinless son of God, chose in total freedom to suffer fully our pains and thus to let us discover the true nature of our own passions. In him, we see and experience the persons we truly are. He who is divine lives our broken humanity not as a curse (Gen. 3:14–19), but as a blessing. His divine compassion makes it possible for us to face our sinful selves, because it transforms our broken human condition from a cause of despair into a source of hope.

✠

Everything that Jesus has done, said, and undergone is meant to show us that the love we most long for is given to us by God, not because we've deserved it, but because God is a God of love.

Jesus has come among us to make that divine love visible and to offer it to us. In his conversation with Nicodemus he says: " . . . this is how God loved the world: he gave his only Son. . . . God sent his Son into the world not to judge the world, but so that through him the world might be saved." In these words the meaning of the Incarnation is summed up. God has become human — that is, God-with-us — in order to show us that the anxious concern for recognition and the violence among us spring from a lack of faith in the love of God. If we had a firm faith in God's unconditional love for us, it would no longer be necessary to be always on the lookout for ways of being admired by people, and we would need, even less, to obtain from people by force what God desires to give us so abundantly.

Prayer

Lord Jesus Christ,
you suffered for us
and left an example
for us to follow in your steps.
You had done nothing wrong,
and had spoken no deceit.
You were insulted
and did not retaliate with insults;
when you were suffering
you made no threats
but put your trust
in the upright judge.

You were bearing our sins
in your own body on the cross,
so that we might die to our sins
and live for uprightness;
through your bruises
we have been healed.

— After 1 Peter 2:21–24

⊰⊱ Saturday in Passion Week ⊰⊱

I shall make a covenant of peace with them, an eternal covenant with them. I shall resettle them and make them grow; I shall set my sanctuary among them for ever. I shall make my home above them; I shall be their God, and they will be my people.

—Ezek. 37:26–27

God cannot be understood; he cannot be grasped by the human mind. The truth escapes our human capacities. The only way to come close to it is by a constant emphasis on the limitations of our human capacities to "have" or "hold" the truth. We can neither explain God nor his presence in history. As soon as we identify God with any specific event or situation, we play God and distort the truth. We only can be faithful in our affirmation that God has not deserted us but calls us in the middle of all the unexplainable absurdities of life. It is very important to be deeply aware of this. There is a great and subtle temptation to suggest to myself or others where God is working and where not, when he is present and when not, but nobody, no Christian, no priest, no monk, has any "special" knowledge about God. God cannot be limited by any human concept or prediction. He is greater than our mind and heart and perfectly free to reveal himself where and when he wants.

✠

We can close our eyes as tightly as we can and clasp our hands as firmly as possible, but God speaks only when he wants to speak. When we realize this our pressing, pushing, and pulling become quite amusing. Sometimes we act

like a child that closes his eyes and thinks that he can make
the world go away.

After having done everything to make some space for
God, it is still God who comes on his own initiative. But we
have a promise upon which to base our hope: The promise
of his love. So our life can rightly be a waiting in expectation, but waiting patiently and with a smile. Then, indeed,
we shall be really surprised and full of joy and gratitude
when he comes.

Prayer

O God, we are the heirs of the covenant
you made with our ancestors
when you told Abraham,
"All the nations of the earth will be blessed
in your descendants."
It was for us that you raised up your servant Jesus
and sent him to bless us.

— After Acts: 3:25–26

⊰ Palm Sunday ⊱

So the disciples went and did as Jesus had told them. They brought the donkey and the colt, then they laid their cloaks on their backs and he took his seat on them. Great crowds of people spread their cloaks on the road, while others were cutting branches from the trees and spreading them in his path. The crowds who went in front of him and those who followed were all shouting:

> *Hosanna to the son of David!*
> *Blessed is he who is coming in the name of the Lord!*
> *Hosanna in the highest heavens!*

—Matt. 21:6–9

✠

Christ on a Donkey, in the Augustiner Museum in Freiburg, is one of the most moving Christ figures I know. . . .

This afternoon I went to the museum to spend some quiet time with this *Christus auf Palmesel* (Christ on palm-donkey).This fourteenth-century sculpture originally comes from Niederrotweil, a small town close to Breisach on the Rhine. It was made to be pulled on a cart in the Palm Sunday procession. . . .

Christ's long, slender face with a high forehead, inward-looking eyes, long hair, and a small forked beard expresses the mystery of his suffering in a way that holds me spellbound. As he rides into Jerusalem surrounded by people shouting "hosanna," "cutting branches from the trees and spreading them in his path" (Matt. 21:8), Jesus appears completely concentrated on something else. He does not look at the excited crowd. He does not wave. He sees beyond all the noise and movement to what is ahead

118

of him: an agonizing journey of betrayal, torture, cruci-
fixion, and death. His unfocused eyes see what nobody
around him can see; his high forehead reflects a knowledge
of things to come far beyond any one's understanding.
There is melancholy, but also peaceful acceptance. There
is insight into the fickleness of the human heart, but also
immense compassion. There is a deep awareness of the
unspeakable pain to be suffered, but also a strong determination to do God's will. Above all, there is love, an endless,
deep, and far-reaching love born from an unbreakable
intimacy with God and reaching out to all people, wherever they are, were, or will be. There is nothing that he
does not fully know. There is nobody whom he does not
fully love.

Every time I look at this Christ on the donkey, I am
reminded again that I am seen by him with all my sins,
guilt, and shame and loved with all his forgiveness, mercy,
and compassion.

Just being with him in the Augustiner Museum is a
prayer. I look and look and look, and I know that he sees
the depths of my heart; I do not have to be afraid.

✠

Joy and sadness are born at the same time, both arising
from such deep places in your heart that you can't find
words to capture your complex emotions.

But this intimate experience in which every bit of life
is touched by a bit of death can point us beyond the
limits of our existence. It can do so by making us look
forward in expectation to the day when our hearts will be
filled with perfect joy, a joy that no one shall take away
from us. Let me therefore now reflect on expectation, first
about expectation as patience, and then about expectation
as joy.

Prayer

Almighty God,
today we pay homage to Christ in his victory.
With songs of praise
we accompany him into his holy city;
grant that we may come
to the heavenly Jerusalem through him
who lives and reigns with you to all eternity.
— From the prayers for the blessing of the palms

❧ Monday in Holy Week ❧

"You have the poor with you always, you will not always have me."

—John 12:8

✠

To choose the little people, the little joys, the little sorrows and to trust that it is there that God will come close — that is the hard way of Jesus. ... Something in me always wants to turn the way of Jesus into a way that is honorable in the eyes of the world. I always want the little way to become the big way. But Jesus' movement toward the places the world wants to move away from cannot be made into a success story.

Every time we think we have touched a place of poverty, we will discover greater poverty beyond that place. There is really no way back to riches, wealth, success, acclaim, and prizes. Beyond physical poverty there is mental poverty, beyond mental poverty there is spiritual poverty, and beyond that there is nothing, nothing but the naked trust that God is mercy.

It is not a way we can walk alone. Only with Jesus can we go to the place where there is nothing but mercy. It is the place from which Jesus cried, "My God, my God, why have you forsaken me?" It is also the place from which Jesus was raised up to new life.

The way of Jesus can be walked only with Jesus. If I want to do it alone, it becomes a form of inverse heroism as fickle as heroism itself. Only Jesus, the Son of God, can walk to that place of total surrender and mercy. He warns us about striking off on our own: "cut off from me, you can

121

do nothing." But he also promises, "Whoever remains in me, with me in him, bears fruit in plenty" (John 15:5).

I now see clearly why action without prayer is so fruitless. It is only in and through prayer that we can become intimately connected with Jesus and find the strength to join him on his way.

✠

Prayer and action, therefore, can never be seen as contradictory or mutually exclusive. Prayer without action grows into powerless pietism, and action without prayer degenerates into questionable manipulation. If prayer leads us into a deeper unity with the compassionate Christ, it will always give rise to concrete acts of service. And if concrete acts of service do indeed lead us to a deeper solidarity with the poor, the hungry, the sick, the dying, and the oppressed, they will always give rise to prayer. In prayer we meet Christ, and in him all human suffering. In service we meet people, and in them the suffering Christ.

Action with and for those who suffer is the concrete expression of the compassionate life and the final criterion of being a Christian. Such acts do not stand beside the moments of prayer and worship but are themselves such moments. Why? Because Jesus Christ, who did not cling to his divinity, but became as we are, can be found where there are hungry, thirsty, alienated, naked, sick, and imprisoned people. Precisely when we live in an ongoing conversation with Christ and allow his Spirit to guide our lives, we will recognize him in the poor, the oppressed, and the downtrodden, and will hear his cry and respond to it wherever he reveals himself....

So worship becomes ministry and ministry becomes worship, and all we say or do, ask for or give, becomes a way to the life in which God's compassion can manifest itself.

Prayer

Rise Yahweh! God, raise your hand,
do not forget the afflicted!
You have seen for yourself the trouble and vexation,
you watch so as to take it in hand.
Yahweh, you listen to the laments of the poor.
You give them courage, you grant them a hearing.

—Ps. 10:12, 14, 17

❧ Tuesday in Holy Week ❧

Jesus was deeply disturbed and declared, "In all truth I tell you, one of you is going to betray me."

✠

Jesus, sitting at table with his disciples, said, "One of you will betray me" (John 13:21)....

As I look more closely at Jesus' words as they are written in Greek, a better translation would be "One of you will hand me over." The term *paradidomi* means "to give over, to hand over, to give into the hands of." It is an important term not only to express what Judas did, but also what God did. Paul writes, " . . . he did not spare his own Son, but 'handed him over' for the sake of all of us" (Rom. 8:32).

If we translate Judas's action as "to betray," as applied to Judas, we do not fully express the mystery because Judas is described as being an instrument of God's work. That is why Jesus said, "The Son of Man is going to his fate, as the scriptures say he will, but alas for the man by whom the Son of Man is betrayed [handed over]" (Matt. 26:24).

This moment when Jesus is handed over to those who do with him as they please is a turning point in Jesus' ministry. It is turning from action to passion. After years of teaching, preaching, healing, and moving to wherever he wanted to go, Jesus is handed over to the caprices of his enemies. Things are now no longer done *by* him, but *to* him. He is flagellated, crowned with thorns, spat at, laughed at, stripped, and nailed naked to a cross. He is a passive victim, subject to other people's actions. From the moment Jesus is handed over, his passion begins, and through this passion he fulfills his vocation.

It is important for me to realize that Jesus fulfills his mission not by what he does, but by what is done to him. Just as with everyone else, most of my life is determined by what is done to me and thus is passion. And because most of my life is passion, things being done to me, only small parts of my life are determined by what I think, say, or do. I am inclined to protest against this and to want all to be action, originated by me. But the truth is that my passion is a much greater part of my life than my action. Not to recognize this is self-deception and not to embrace my passion with love is self-rejection.

It is good news to know that Jesus is handed over to passion, and through his passion accomplishes his divine task on earth. It is good news for a world passionately searching for wholeness.

Jesus' words to Peter remind me that Jesus' transition from action to passion must also be ours if we want to follow his way. He says, "When you were young you put on your own belt and walked where you liked; but when you grow old you will stretch out your hands, and somebody else will put a belt round you and take you where you would rather not go' (John 21:18).

I, too, have to let myself be "handed over" and thus fulfill my vocation.

Prayer

If you, O God, are for us,
who can be against us?
Since you did not spare your own Son,
but gave him up for the sake of all of us,
then can we not expect that with him
you will freely give us all his gifts?
Are we not sure that it is Christ Jesus,
your Son, who died —
yes and more, who was raised from the dead
and is at God's right hand —
and who is adding his plea for us?

— After Rom. 8:31–32, 34

✠ Wednesday in Holy Week ✠

Go to a certain man in the city and say to him, "The Master says: My time is near. It is at your house that I am keeping Passover with my disciples." The disciples did what Jesus told them and prepared the Passover.

—Matt. 26:18–19

✠

O Lord, how can I ever go anywhere else but to you to find the love I so desire! How can I expect from people as sinful as myself a love that can touch me in the most hidden corners of my being? Who can wash me clean as you do and give me food and drink as you do? Who wants me to be so close, so intimate and so safe as you do? O Lord, your love is not an intangible love, a love that remains words and thoughts. No, Lord, your love is a love that comes from your human heart. It is a heart-felt love that expresses itself through your whole being. You speak . . . you look . . . you touch . . . you give me food. Yes, you make your love a love that reaches all the senses of my body and holds me as a mother holds her child, embraces me as a father embraces his son, and touches me as a brother touches his sister and brother.

✠

Lord Jesus, I look at you, and my eyes are fixed on your eyes. Your eyes penetrate the eternal mystery of the divine and see the glory of God. They are also the eyes that saw Simon, Andrew, Nathanael, and Levi, the eyes that saw the woman with a hemorrhage, the widow of Nain, the blind, the lame, the lepers, and the hungry crowd, the eyes that saw the sad, rich ruler, the fearful disciples on the lake, and the sorrowful women at the tomb. Your eyes, O Lord,

see in one glance the inexhaustible love of God and the
seemingly endless agony of all people who have lost faith
in that love and are like sheep without a shepherd.

As I look into your eyes, they frighten me because they
pierce like flames of fire my innermost being, but they con-
sole me as well, because these flames are purifying and
healing. Your eyes are so severe yet so loving, so unmask-
ing yet so protecting, so penetrating yet so caressing, so
profound yet so intimate, so distant yet so inviting.

I gradually realize that I want to be seen by you, to dwell
under your caring gaze, and to grow strong and gentle in
your sight. Lord, let me see what you see — the love of God
and the suffering of people so that my eyes may become
more and more like yours, eyes that can heal wounded
hearts.

Prayer

Dear Lord,
your disciple Peter wanted to know
who would betray you.
You pointed to Judas but a little later also to him.
Judas betrayed, Peter denied you.
Judas hanged himself,
Peter became the apostle
whom you made the first among equals.
Lord, give me faith,
faith in your endless mercy,
your boundless forgiveness,
your unfathomable goodness.
Let me not be tempted to think that my sins
are too great to be forgiven,
too abominable to be touched by your mercy.
Let me never run away from you
but return to you again and again,

asking you to be my Lord,
my Shepherd, my Stronghold, and my Refuge.
Take me under your wing, O Lord,
and let me know that you do not reject me
as long as I keep asking you to forgive me.
Perhaps my doubt in your forgiveness is a greater sin
than the sins I consider too great to be forgiven.
Perhaps I make myself too important, too great
when I think
that I cannot be embraced by you any more.
Lord, look at me, accept my prayer
as you accepted Peter's prayer,
and let me not run away from you
in the night as Judas did.

Bless me, Lord, in this Holy Week,
and give me the grace
to know your loving presence more intimately.

Amen.

*Jesus . . . removed his outer garments and, taking a towel,
wrapped it round his waist; he then poured water into a basin
and began to wash the disciples' feet and to wipe them with
the towel he was wearing. . . .*

*[He said], "I have given you an example so that you may
copy what I have done to you."*

— John 13:4–5, 15

✠

Just before entering on the road of his passion he washed
the feet of his disciples and offered them his body and
blood as food and drink. These two acts belong together.
They are both an expression of God's determination to
show us the fullness of his love. Therefore John intro-
duces the story of the washing of the disciples' feet with
the words: "Jesus . . . having loved those who were his in
the world, loved them to the end" (John 13:1).

What is even more astonishing is that on both occasions Jesus commands us to do the same. After washing
his disciples' feet, Jesus says, "I have given you an example so that you may copy what I have done to you"(John
13:15). After giving himself as food and drink, he says, "Do
this in remembrance of me" (Luke 22:19). Jesus calls us to
continue his mission of revealing the perfect love of God
in this world. He calls us to total self-giving. He does not
want us to keep anything for ourselves. Rather, he wants
our love to be as full, as radical, and as complete as his
own. He wants us to bend ourselves to the ground and
touch the places in each other that most need washing. He
also wants us to say to each other, "Eat of me and drink

of me." By this complete mutual nurturing, he wants us to become one body and one spirit, united by the love of God.

✠

I am looking at you, Lord. You have said so many loving words. Your heart has spoken so clearly. Now you want to show me even more clearly how much you love me. Knowing that your Father has put everything in your hands, that you have come from God and are returning to God, you remove your outer garments and, taking a towel, you wrap it around your waist, pour water into a basin and begin to wash my feet, and then wipe them with the towel you are wearing....

You look at me with utter tenderness, saying, "I want you to be with me. I want you to have a full share in my life. I want you to belong to me as much as I belong to my Father. I want to wash you completely clean so that you and I can be one and so that you can do to others what I have done to you."

I am looking at you again, Lord. You stand up and invite me to the table. As we are eating, you take bread, say the blessing, break the bread, and give it to me. "Take and eat," you say, "this is my body given for you." Then you take a cup, and, after giving thanks, you hand it to me, saying, "This is my blood, the blood of the new covenant poured out for you." Knowing that your hour has come to pass from this world to your Father and having loved me, you now love me to the end. You give me everything that you have and are. You pour out for me your very self. All the love that you carry for me in your heart now becomes manifest. You wash my feet and then give me your own body and blood as food and drink.

O Lord, how can I ever go anywhere else but to you to find the love I so desire!

✠

Every time you celebrate the Eucharist and receive the
bread and wine, the body and blood of Jesus, his suffering
and his death become a suffering and death for you. Passion becomes compassion, for you. You are incorporated
into Jesus. You become part of his "body" and in that most
compassionate way are freed from your deepest solitude.
Through the Eucharist you come to belong to Jesus in the
most intimate way, to him who has suffered for you, died
for you and rose again so that you may suffer, die, and rise
again with him.

Prayer

Almighty, everlasting God,
on the evening before he suffered
your beloved son entrusted to the Church
the sacrifice of the new and eternal covenant
and founded the banquet of his love.
Grant that from this mystery
we may receive the fullness of life and love.
We ask this through Jesus Christ.

✠ Good Friday ✠

After Jesus had taken the wine he said, "It is fulfilled"; and
bowing his head he gave up his spirit....
   One of the soldiers pierced his side with a lance; and im-
mediately there came out blood and water. This is the evidence
of one who saw it — true evidence, and he knows that what he
says is true — and he gives it so that you may believe as well.
Because all this happened to fulfil the words of scripture:...
   They will look to the one whom they have pierced.

—John 19:30, 34–37

✠

Good Friday: day of the cross, day of suffering, day of hope,
day of abandonment, day of victory, day of mourning, day
of joy, day of endings, day of beginnings.

   During the liturgy at Trosly, Père Thomas and Père
Gilbert...took the huge cross that hangs behind the altar from the wall and held it so that the whole community
could come and kiss the dead body of Christ. They all
came, more than four hundred people — handicapped
men and women and their assistants and friends. Everybody seemed to know very well what they were doing:
expressing their love and gratitude for him who gave his
life for them. As they were crowding around the cross and
kissing the feet and the head of Jesus, I closed my eyes and
could see his sacred body stretched out and crucified upon
our planet earth. I saw the immense suffering of humanity during the centuries: people killing each other; people
dying from starvation and epidemics; people driven from
their homes; people sleeping on the streets of large cities;
people clinging to each other in desperation; people flagellated, tortured, burned, and mutilated; people alone in

locked flats, in prison dungeons, in labor camps; people craving a gentle word, a friendly letter, a consoling embrace, people . . . all crying out with an anguished voice: "My God, my God, why have you forsaken us?"

Imagining the naked, lacerated body of Christ stretched out over our globe, I was filled with horror. But as I opened my eyes I saw Jacques, who bears the marks of suffering in his face, kiss the body with passion and tears in his eyes. I saw Ivan carried on Michael's back. I saw Edith coming in her wheelchair. As they came — walking or limping, seeing or blind, hearing or deaf — I saw the endless procession of humanity gathering around the sacred body of Jesus, covering it with their tears and their kisses, and slowly moving away from it comforted and consoled by such great love. . . . With my mind's eye I saw the huge crowds of isolated, agonizing individuals walking away from the cross together, bound by the love they had seen with their own eyes and touched with their own lips. The cross of horror became the cross of hope, the tortured body became the body that gives new life; the gaping wounds became the source of forgiveness, healing, and reconciliation.

Prayer

O dear Lord, what can I say to you?
Is there any word that could come from my mouth,
any thought? any sentence?
You died for me, you gave all for my sins,
you not only became man for me
but also suffered the most cruel death for me.
Is there any response?
I wish that I could find a fitting response,
but in contemplating your Holy Passion and Death
I can only confess humbly to you

that the immensity of your divine love
makes any response seem totally inadequate.
Let me just stand and look at you.
Your body is broken, your head wounded,
your hands and feet are split open by nails,
your side is pierced.
Your dead body now rests in the arms of your Mother.
It is all over now. It is finished.
It is fulfilled. It is accomplished.
Sweet Lord, gracious Lord,
generous Lord, forgiving Lord,
I adore you, I praise you, I thank you.
You have made all things new
through your passion and death.
Your cross has been planted in this world
as the new sign of hope.

Let me always live under your cross, O Lord,
and proclaim the hope of your cross unceasingly.
Amen.

⊰ Holy Saturday ⊱

You cannot have forgotten that all of us, when we were bap-
tized into Christ Jesus, were baptized into his death. So by our
baptism into his death we were buried with him.... But we
believe that, if we died with Christ, then we shall live with
him too.

—Rom. 6:3, 4, 8

✠

If the God who revealed life to us, and whose only desire
is to bring us to life, loved us so much that he wanted to experience with us the total absurdity of death, then — yes,
then there must be hope; then there must be something
more than death; then there must be a promise that is not
fulfilled in our short existence in this world; then leaving
behind the ones you love, the flowers and the trees, the
mountains and the oceans, the beauty of art and music,
and all the exuberant gifts of life cannot be just the destruction and cruel end of all things; then indeed we have
to wait for the third day.

✠

But mortification — literally, "making death" — is what
life is all about, a slow discovery of the mortality of all
that is created so that we can appreciate its beauty without
clinging to it as if it were a lasting possession. Our lives
can indeed be seen as a process of becoming familiar with
death, as a school in the art of dying. I do not mean this in a
morbid way. On the contrary, when we see life constantly
relativized by death, we can enjoy it for what it is: a free
gift. The pictures, letters, and books of the past reveal life to
us as a constant saying of farewell to beautiful places, good
people, and wonderful experiences. Look at the pictures of

your children when you could play with them on the floor
of the living room. How quickly you had to say goodbye to
them! Look at the snapshots of your bike trips with mother
in Brittany in the mid-thirties. How few were the summers
in which those trips were possible! Read mother's letters
when you were in Amalfi recuperating from your illness
and my letters to you from my first trip to England. They
speak now of fleeting moments. Look at the wedding pictures of your children and at the Bible I gave you on the
day of my ordination. All these times have passed by like
friendly visitors, leaving you with dear memories but also
with the sad recognition of the shortness of life. In every
arrival there is a leave-taking; in every reunion there is a
separation; in each one's growing up there is a growing old;
in every smile there is a tear; and in every success there is a
loss. All living is dying and all celebration is mortification
too.

Prayer

I call to you, Yahweh, all day.
I stretch out my hands to you.

Do you work wonders for the dead,
can shadows rise up to praise you?
Do they speak in the grave of your faithful love,
of your constancy in the place of perdition?
Are your wonders known in the darkness,
your saving justice in the land of oblivion?

But, for my part. I cry to you, Yahweh,
every morning my prayer comes before you.

—Ps. 88:9–13

⚜ Easter Sunday ⚜

The tradition I handed on to you in the first place, a tradition which I had myself received, was that Christ died for our sins, in accordance with the scriptures, and that he was buried; and that on the third day, he was raised to life, in accordance with the scriptures; and that he appeared to Cephas; and later to the Twelve; and next he appeared to more than five hundred of the brothers at the same time.... This is what we preach and what you believed.

—1 Cor. 15:3–6, 11

✠

Easter vigil. The Lord is risen indeed. They shouted it in French, German, English, Spanish, Portuguese, Italian, Dutch, and Arabic. There were bells, alleluias, smiles, laughter, and a deep sense that there is hope. This community of handicapped people and their assistants was loudly proclaiming that Christ's body did not remain in the tomb, but was raised to new life, and that our own bodies will join him in glory.

While all this joy was filling the chapel, I saw that Nathan stood up with Philippe in his arms and left the church. Philippe's body is severely distorted. He cannot speak, walk, dress, or feed himself and needs help every second of his waking hours. He had been lying in an assistant's lap, quietly sleeping. But when the celebration became more lively he started to howl, an anguished howl coming from deep down in his being....

When I saw Philippe in Nathan's arms I suddenly realized what we were proclaiming on this Easter vigil. Philippe's body is a body destined to a new life, a resurrected life. In his new body he will carry the signs of his

suffering, just as Jesus carried the wounds of the crucifix-
ion into his glory. And yet he will no longer be suffering,
· but will join the saints around the altar of the lamb.

Still, the celebration of the resurrection of the body is
also the celebration of the daily care given to the bodies of these handicapped men and women. Washing and
feeding, pushing wheelchairs, carrying, kissing, and caressing — these are all ways in which these broken bodies
are made ready for the moment of a new life. Not only their
wounds but also the care given them will remain visible
in the resurrection.

It is a great and powerful mystery. Philippe's poor distorted body will one day be buried and return to dust. But
he will rise again on the day of the resurrection of the dead.
He will rise from the grave with a new body and will show
gloriously the pain he suffered and the love he received.
It will not be just *a* body. It will be *his* body, a new body, a
body that can be touched but is no longer subject to torture
and destruction. His passion will be over.

What a faith! What a hope! What a love! The body is not
a prison to escape from, but a temple in which God already
dwells, and in which God's glory will be fully manifested
on the day of the resurrection.

✠

Easter season is a time of hope. There still is fear, there still
is a painful awareness of sinfulness, but there also is light
breaking through. Something new is happening, something that goes beyond the changing moods of our life.
We can be joyful or sad, optimistic or pessimistic, tranquil
or angry, but the solid stream of God's presence moves
deeper than the small waves of our minds and hearts.
Easter brings the awareness that God is present even when
his presence is not directly noticed. Easter brings the good
news that, although things seem to get worse in the world,
the Evil One has already been overcome. Easter allows us

to affirm that although God seems very distant and although we remain preoccupied with many little things, our Lord walks with us on the road and keeps explaining the Scriptures to us. Thus there are many rays of hope casting their light on our way through life.

Prayer

Almighty, everlasting God,
on this day
you conquered death through your son
and opened for us the path to eternal life.
And so we celebrate in joy
the feast of his resurrection.
Make us new through your Spirit,
so that we too may rise
and walk in the light of life.
We ask this through Jesus Christ.

✦ Sources ✦

Abbreviations

Ash Wednesday / FIRST SELECTION: Road 137; SECOND SELECTION: Cry 55

Thursday after Ash Wednesday / FIRST: translated from Nachts bricht der Tag an 86; SECOND: Letters 52–53

Friday after Ash Wednesday / FIRST: Letters 36, 40; SECOND: Reaching Out 128–30

Saturday after Ash Wednesday / FIRST: Making 50–51; SECOND: Making 56–57

First Sunday in Lent / FIRST: Living Reminder 30–32; SECOND: Road 120–21; PRAYER: Road 121

Monday of the First Week / FIRST: Reaching Out 66–67; SECOND: Reaching Out 102–3; PRAYER: Cry 66–67

Tuesday of the First Week / FIRST: Way of the Heart 72, 75; SECOND: Letters 76–77; THIRD: With Open Hands 56; PRAYER: Cry 26–27

Wednesday of the First Week / FIRST: Gracias 47–48; SECOND: Gracias 50

Thursday of the First Week / FIRST: Making 45–47; SECOND: Making 50–51

Friday of the First Week / FIRST: Road 67–68; SECOND: Letters 54

Saturday of the First Week / FIRST: Compassion 110–11; SECOND: Letters 47–48; PRAYER: Cry 103

Second Sunday in Lent / FIRST: Compassion 113; SECOND: Letters 36–37; THIRD: Letters 47

Monday of the Second Week / FIRST: *Compassion* 20–21; SECOND: *Compassion* 4; PRAYER: *Cry* 62–63

Tuesday of the Second Week / FIRST: *Compassion* 28–29; SECOND: *Letters* 41–43

Wednesday of the Second Week / FIRST: *Compassion* 27–28; SECOND: *Compassion* 31; THIRD: *Compassion* 32

Thursday of the Second Week / FIRST: *Out of Solitude* 17–19; SECOND: *Out of Solitude* 21–22

Friday of the Second Week / FIRST: *Creative Ministry* 27–28; SECOND: *Creative Ministry* 88–89

Saturday of the Second Week / FIRST: *Road* 72–73; SECOND: *Road* 157–58

Third Sunday in Lent / FIRST: *Cry* 56; SECOND: *Letters* 57–58

Monday of the Third Week / FIRST: *Letters* 65, 66; SECOND: *Letters* 67–68; PRAYER: *Cry* 96–97

Tuesday of the Third Week / FIRST: *Compassion* 23–24; SECOND: *Compassion* 133–34; PRAYER: *Cry* 74–75

Wednesday of the Third Week / FIRST: *Living Reminder* 47–50; SECOND: *Gracias* 125

Thursday of the Third Week / FIRST: *Making* 65–66; SECOND: *Making* 67–68

Friday of the Third Week / FIRST: *Genesee Diary* 152; PRAYER: *Cry* 98

Saturday of the Third Week / FIRST: *Making* 57–59; PRAYER: *Cry* 64–65

Fourth Sunday in Lent / FIRST: *Way of the Heart* 22–23; SECOND: *Way of the Heart* 24–26; THIRD: *Letters* 68

Monday of the Fourth Week / FIRST: *Letters* 52; SECOND: *Compassion* 18

Tuesday of the Fourth Week / FIRST: *Road* 120; SECOND: *Genesee Diary* 57–58; PRAYER: *Cry* 24–25

Wednesday of the Fourth Week / FIRST: *Making* 47–50; SECOND: *Road* 146–47

Thursday of the Fourth Week / FIRST: *Road* 97; SECOND: *Road* 98; PRAYER: *Cry* 34–35

Friday of the Fourth Week / FIRST: *Compassion* 40–41; SECOND: *Genesee Diary* 157

Saturday of the Fourth Week / FIRST: *Road* 147–48; PRAYER: *Cry* 66–67

Passion Sunday: FIRST: *Letters* 25–26; SECOND: translated from *Gebete aus der Stille* 61–62; PRAYER: *Cry* 74–75

Monday in Passion Week / FIRST: *Compassion* 18, 13, 15; SECOND: *Compassion* 15–16

Tuesday in Passion Week / FIRST: *Way of the Heart* 58–59, 60–61; SECOND: *Out of Solitude* 25–26; THIRD: *Gracias* 183; FOURTH: *Gracias* 49

Wednesday in Passion Week / FIRST: *Making* 52–56; SECOND: *Gracias* 133; PRAYER: *Cry* 132

Thursday in Passion Week / FIRST: *Gracias* 56; SECOND: *Letters* 75–76

Friday in Passion Week / FIRST: *Compassion* 17; SECOND: *Letters* 57–58

Saturday in Passion Week / FIRST: *Genesee Diary* 116–17; SECOND: *Genesee Diary* 108–9

Palm Sunday: FIRST: *Road* 134–35; SECOND: *Out of Solitude* 52–53

Monday in Holy Week / FIRST: *Road* 88–89; SECOND: *Compassion* 116–17; THIRD: *Compassion* 120–21

Tuesday in Holy Week / FIRST: *Road* 155–56

Wednesday in Holy Week / FIRST: *Heart Speaks to Heart* 28–29; SECOND: *Road* 56; PRAYER: *Cry* 76–77

Holy Thursday / FIRST: *Road* 159; SECOND: *Heart Speaks to Heart* 26–28; THIRD: *Letters* 31

Good Friday / FIRST: *Road* 160–61; PRAYER: *Cry* 78–79

Holy Saturday / FIRST: *Letter of Consolation* 78; SECOND: *Letter of Consolation* 42–43

Easter Sunday / FIRST: *Road* 162–63; SECOND: *Cry* 85